Digital Marketing

UPGRADE 2020

Tips for Keeping Up With Social Media News & Trends

By

DOUGLAS WELCH

© Copyright 2020 by DOUGLAS WELCH

All rights reserved.

This document is geared towards providing exact and reliable information with regards to the topic and issue covered. The publication is sold with the idea that the publisher is not required to render accounting, officially permitted, or otherwise, qualified services. If advice is necessary, legal or professional, a practiced individual in the profession should be ordered.

- From a Declaration of Principles which was accepted and approved equally by a Committee of the American Bar Association and a Committee of Publishers and Associations.

In no way is it legal to reproduce, duplicate, or transmit any part of this document in either electronic means or in printed format. Recording of this publication is strictly prohibited and any storage of this document is not allowed unless with written permission from the publisher. All rights reserved.

The information provided herein is stated to be truthful and consistent, in that any liability, in terms of inattention or otherwise, by any usage or abuse of any policies, processes, or directions contained within is the solitary and utter responsibility of the recipient reader. Under no circumstances will any legal responsibility or blame be held against the publisher for any reparation, damages, or monetary loss due to the information herein, either directly or indirectly.

Respective authors own all copyrights not held by the publisher.

The information herein is offered for informational purposes solely, and is universal as so. The presentation of the information is without contract or any type of guarantee assurance.

The trademarks that are used are without any consent, and the publication of the trademark is without permission or backing by the trademark owner. All trademarks and brands within this book are for clarifying purposes only and are the owned by the owners themselves, not affiliated with this document

Table Of Content

Copyright 2

Introduction 5

Chapter One

Ways to Boost Your Business Profits With Digital Marketing 7

Digital Marketing to Promote Businesses to Greater Heights of Success 12

Great Ways Digital Marketing Can Help Your Business 13

Digital Marketing Trends for 2020 you Should Know 16

Effective Digital Marketing Tactics and Strategies in 2020 and Beyond 23

Chapter Two

Using a Digital Marketing Strategy to Increase Marketing Impact 30

Tips for Implementing A Solid Digital Marketing Strategy 34

Ways to Improve Your Digital Marketing Strategy 36

Reasons Why You Should Have a Digital Marketing Strategy 39

Fresh Aspects That One Should Know About Digital Marketing 43

Chapter Three

When You Should Change Your Digital Marketing Strategy 47

Common Misconceptions About Digital Marketing 48

Amazing Benefits And Importance of Digital Marketing For Growth 51

Why Your Business Needs Digital Marketing Services 55

Tips to Start a Career in Digital Marketing 57

The Top Digital Marketing Trends That Are Transforming Businesses 60

Chapter Four

Costly Digital Marketing Mistakes to Avoid in 2020 66

key factors make digital marketing plan successful 69

Reasons How a Digital Marketing Program Can Help You 72

Skills to Become a Rockstar in Digital Marketing 74

The Main Concerns With Digital Marketing to the Mass Market 79

Chapter Five

Ways Digital Has Changed Business Forever 82

The Scope of Digital Marketing in 2020 88

Tips on How Digital Marketing Can Increase Your Revenue 92

Smart Ways for Bringing New Life To Your Business 94

Marketing Lessons to Succeed in 2020 97

Conclusion 104

Introduction

Digital marketing is actually one of the fastest growing advertising sectors. Nonetheless, marketers need to do more than expand their advertising digitally into the digital marketing area to keep up with the massive impact it puts on mainstream business practice.

Digital marketing covers all marketing campaigns using an electronic device or the Internet. Organizations use digital channels for connection to current and potential clients such as search engines, social media, e-mail and other Web sites.

Digital marketing introduces new standards to customer-brand commitment; it also forms advertising technologies in new and old ways. Evidence has shown that even while watching television, the most prominent and important users continue to engage in digital media. To be truly successful, the marketing strategy of a company must be integrated from the outset of digital marketing.

Rocket science isn't internet marketing. There are no restrictions. Digital marketing is, as you can see, a big and complicated topic. Digital commercialisation is a big topic and in 30 hours you can't make a hero! It is a method of marketing technique in which advertisement is carried out by means of internet networks and platforms. For addition to traditional TV and radio, the internet is used as a major advertising medium.

The sector is one of the fastest growing, so there is a great deal of room for growth and development. Since 2009, it has been one of the top five rising markets. It is essentially advertising by digital marketing outlets of goods, services or brands. It's much more sophisticated than the traditional marketing approach because you have to be very selective to choose the right strategy.

You will differentiate yourself from others within the company and get your own digital advertising and marketing platform to stand out when talking to an influencer or potential employer. The perfect influencers in ads are people who talk and show themselves to others.

You can incorporate elements of all 3 channels into your digital advertising strategy, and all work together to help you attain your target. There are many facets to an intelligent and powerful digital marketing campaign. You will then have a fully integrated approach for digital marketing and advertising.

A digital marketing and advertising strategy does not have to be difficult to develop. Your digital marketing plan may include multiple targets depending on your organization's size, so getting back to this simple way of thinking about tactics will allow you to remain focused on achieving these goals. This must provide the right content on the basis of its purchasing process. New consumers and new customers are motivated to become committed to a clearly defined digital marketing and advertising plan.

You must create a marketing system that focuses on a group or groups of people. Developing the advertising program with the highest intentions is the key problem. Thankfully, in the last few decades targeting tech has been very far-reaching, and many technologies can support. Ask questions before you choose a new advertising and marketing tool. You must learn how to best use modern tools and techniques for a successful campaign. In other words, digital tools and expertise have a powerful capacity to build profits, and businesses want to use that strength to sustain profitability.

Over recent decades, the use of digital radiography has grown rapidly. You can also use advanced email marketing tools to execute tailored promotions to convince the customers to perform such things such as registering for courses, the purchasing of your products, attending an event or anyway. This demonstrates how to use social networking resources like Instagram, podcasting and blogging by using email marketing, web affiliate marketing, Facebook marketing.

The unity of every area of life and in digital marketing plays a very important role. Many owners of companies tend to be successful at first, but gradually get exhausted over time. Those who market their products efficiently over longer periods of time would benefit further.

Digital Marketing UPGRADE 2020

CHAPTER ONE

Ways to Boost Your Business Profits With Digital Marketing

Have you ever wondered if your favorite collection will be viewed by you, after which the advertising of the same collection will also be received on another online platform? Somehow you can fail to purchase an item and a few minutes later an email says "You have an unsheet item in your cart." You have ever wondered why there are so many websites linked to same firms, but why do only a few of them appear on Google's first search page? There are many things you can think about, but only a few are sure how this intangible phenomenon can exist. Digital marketing is the key to all these "you've still" questions.

Digital Marketing has become the sensation and the hope of this century for all types of companies. It is a collection of marketing tools and tactics to help the products and services via the Web. PROFIT and digital marketing really help to make it possible, from small companies to big businesses, have the same agenda for their success. Businessmen and advertisers know the world as its clients on the digitalization road.

Therefore, they can't just follow the forms that customers are highly appreciated and recommended. Internet marketing sometimes referred to as digital marketing

1. Create your presence online

The main task is to create your company online. You can display the company through Web sites and social media platforms, also known as Business Branding. It provides the biggest platform to work on in this environment of more than 465 million highly active internet users. In fact, smartphone is another advanced technology that makes it easy for users to gather and buy information about products or services.

Therefore, you will take on the Internet's strength that can render your business magical. Creating your own website and listing organizations on various social media platforms if you want to see any significant progress. Therefore, don't forget to answer all the comments and requests on the online platforms listed. The solution helps to make a good impression on each of them.

2. Get the Social Media Advertising Advertisements

Registering your brand on paying advertisements, including Facebook Ads, Instagram Ads, LinkedIn ads, and many others, is the fastest and most powerful way to get your company visible. For starters, there are already 2,6 billion active Facebook users looking for new and reliable sources when we just talk about Facebook. Statistically, on social media feedback and commentaries more than 25% of online social media time and 60% of online purchases are made. Such numbers clearly show how much exposure the company can obtain from social media.

Facebook offers various kinds of marketing, whether you just want more "likes" for your new product or service or use them as a conversion tool.

In the same way, as we think about Instagram, the younger generation of over 700 million active users have flocked to this social media platform. The advertisers are gradually able to share their ads using filtered images. Instagram is one of the natural methods for posting the brand's content.

3. Pay by click

PPC is the ideal platform for purchases and requests. If you do not follow PPC strategy, at least 10-15% of people who click on sponsored ads that lose their company. Most PPC companies offer services to manage the PPC program if you are not happy with managing the camps or are able to employ PPC specialists with them.

This is critical, because Google Adwords is the best friend of your PPC specialist, as it delivers a variety of options, ranging from good old search to video and re-marketing.

This platform offers the client a wide range of options to meet millions of potential clients easily by following the patterns of the PPC campaigns.

4. SEO

Optimization of the search engine is one of the underrated and worthwhile marketing tactics that has ignited the marketers ' nerves. SEO is advertising based marketing to improve the traffic and revenue of natural products. It is the fastest but not the paying way or the cheapest online marketing strategy that lets the business hit places that you never thought possible.

According to the report, 75% of Google apps will never go past page 1, which ensures that if you don't get the top ten, you won't get the exposure you need for revenue. Even if you can make use of SEO tools in organic search.

5. Making and posting the video content

Video nowadays is the main way for you to share the message of your brand. More than 5 hours are spent online watching and purchasing video content. This offers advertisers a confidence that 69% of all internet traffic will be accounted for in 2020, mobile video ads will rise five times faster than desktops and web landing pages, with 800% more conversion, which is massive and also sensible.

You may find many businesses who believe and want to communicate their brand message through video content instead of text as video content offers more imagery and human touch than any other technique of content sharing.

6. Digital Social Media Marketing Additional Focus

Facebook, a social media giant, has officially released an estimated 556 million active digital daily users, indicating an annually growth of 49 percent. It converts into 945 million internet monthly active users, which shows an increase in users by 39 percent year on year.

This is clearly an indicator of the influence of mobile social media marketing that should lead to more content being created in line with the patterns in social media and local advertising targeted at mobile social media users. Mobile phones are now the basic means of contact and are also the perfect source of advertising.

7. Ramp up email marketing

There is more to it than email just meant for official communication. The more proactive and focused you are, the greater the conversions. For example, you have a lot of information about your clients in your Ecommerce company and you can benefit from it. You would hate a shopping cart that was dumped, but how do you reverse this trend? You will continue remarketing (a principle in digital marketing) by e-mailing the items that are left in the basket.

Email Marketing helps cause an email series once a cart is removed, which results in more sales. There are a total of three e-mails, one sent directly, another 24 hours later and one week back. The most effective. It also acts as a consumer backup source.

8. Content Generation

If you wish to increase the visibility of your brand, you will produce appropriate company or promotional content to educate your clients or viewers. The contents are available in any type; forums, video clipboards, testimonials, interviews, material of the website, graphics, images, etc.

If you want to see your content and to become more popular, begin by adding content to other blogs in similar fields. The advertising is considered good when the right message is sent to millions of consumers ' hearts and minds. But the quality of your company is largely determined by the kind of content that you share with your end users, which is often ignored by advertisers.

9. Track your behavior and achievement

Exploring various digital marketing tactics is a good thing, but if you don't track your contributions and promotions it will not benefit. Consider evaluating what you can do to change it after testing. By which apps more traffic is being made available. What should your area of focus be? When you dream of a big business, all these results are really significant. You will, for example, discover how and what people are finding their stores on arrival from Google research and search consoles.

The age, location, relationship status, preferences and actions of your fans and customers is demonstrated by Facebook Insights and Ad Manager. Listening apps for social media will inform us what consumers and other issues are important to our business and our goods. To get a better understanding of what is important and interesting, use these resources for gain insights into your audience's demographic and psychography profiles.

10. Virtual PR

By adopting a virtual Marketing campaign you will draw on the credibility of your company. You might just submit a story in your business or feature a CEO on blog posts if you visit different media-related websites and give them over a strong pitch. The more people talk about your business, tweet your company, and discuss your name, the greater your exposure for the next year.

Digital Marketing to Promote Businesses to Greater Heights of Success

You, your rivals, your end-users and your staff, everyone is interactive. You are physical. Many or almost all of the resources are open to everyone. But not everyone can use these devices optimally, nor do they know how to do it work for their organizations. The full digital Marketing Course is therefore a good idea, because in this extremely dynamic environment it gives you an advantage. You will hit new heights for your company when you receive the digital marketing credential.

- ✓ **Be Present and Standard:** Anywhere you can have an online presence. Have your company or all social media channels. Have your business. You don't know which one will take the speed and which will be your next choice of buyers. Note to create a profile on every forum. Remember to keep periodically on the digital media platforms with your contact. This is likely to follow your potential consumer base. Make sure the new data are available from your end.
- ✓ **Have a website that works:** Make sure that you invest in a nice, scalable website. Perhaps you don't use it actually for all of your services or products. It doesn't matter how big the company is. Many organizations neglect this dimension, which needs to be addressed. Hold your job, customer feedback and communications up to date. There are still many customer enquiries obtained from many companies on their websites. It can therefore be a powerful digital space to extend your company.
- ✓ **Understand and Apply the Terminology:** Words like SEO might seem unfamiliar or ambiguous to you. Ununderstand and apply jargon. Nonetheless, you need to understand them better or hire a professional marketer. It is not difficult to use digital marketing for corporate advertising, but it needs time, commitment and experience. Make sure all of these are available.

- ✓ **Use Content Marketing:** Most businesses use digital marketing strategies only for social media. It does include content Marketing in its truest form, though, by websites or forums or digital platforms, for instance, that your consumers may have like your guests.

These are some ideas to get your **digital marketing campaign** going. You will see the impact on your company overall success when you continue doing so in a prepared and consistent manner.

Great Ways Digital Marketing Can Help Your Business

Since modern technological advances are quick, companies do their best to remain in the race. It is a matter of sinking or floating today to have a good digital marketing campaign. This makes a difference to succeed or fail an organization.

Even with a lot of traffic on your web, if your guests don't turn to consumers it doesn't mean anything for your business. The best opportunity for businesses to succeed, thrive and expand are digital marketing strategies and tools. These are the ways the company can be positively helped by digital marketing.

- ✓ *This helps you to communicate with a target audience.* The technologies that help you to connect with a targeted audience in real time are one of the main advantage of digital marketing versus traditional marketing. When you engage with your customers, your clients expect you to connect with them. The way you treat these relationships distinguishes between success and failure.

You can also gain a better understanding of what your target audience is after when engaging with your clients. You will benefit from this insight by making the right decisions, optimizing the company interactions and creating customer relationships to create brand loyalty.

Digital marketing is an excellent strategic approach that leading people to take steps which support your company or brand. This drives your customers into action. Transformation from user to customer is in the hands of the viewer of your site. It is, however, up to the digital marketer to have the guests transform using knowledge and creative tactics.

- ✓ *Calls-to-action (CTA-s)* is one of the most effective ways to do this. A CTA motivates the guests to do what they want: sign, purchase, update, and so forth. It is a button composed of keywords for behavior that encourage the user to do as he or she asks for and display the psychological effect that can have a particular color. The color scheme, visuals and even the location on the web can all represent.
- ✓ *it has become an area for online play:* digital marketing has for some time been a luxury for large corporations with enough resources to support such a marketing campaign. Digital marketing plays a role in allowing medium-sized and small firms to compete with big corporations, drawing more limited traffic.

Small and medium-sized businesses now have the ability to manufacture and market their products as large enterprises might not. This gives them the opportunity to connect with consumers around the globe, even where they have no offices or physical shops.

- ✓ *it serves for internet consumers:* today, mobile Internet, with its rapid rise in smartphones and tablets, has dominated Desktop users in terms of being the principal source of information and an important form of communication. To order to help your business growth, it is more important than ever that you have a digital marketing campaign focused on mobile consumers.

Mobile phones are no longer simply replacements to computers and laptops, but are also one of the major factors in attracting your customers in that they can gain or lose a potential customer.

- ✓ *It takes you to conversions:* the amount of traffic that is turned into leads and sales is reflected in the profitability of your market. If your guests don't turn the way you expect them, both your advertising and publicity efforts are worthless. This is why optimization of conversion is so critical.

  Many approaches and resources are available, such as search engine optimization, email marketing and social media marketing, that can improve significantly the digital marketing strategy. SEO Sydney experts say that visiting your website is a first move for a customer and it is important for your clicks to appear on the first page of the Google results.

- ✓ *The brand credibility builds:* the traffic your digital marketing campaign draws is made up of an audience who presumably wants to find out more about your brand and to buy what you have to sell. If you are a company that delivers as you say, you should build a quality relationship with your customer and help them move their website daily, from curious travelers to committed customers.

  This must draw on the credibility of your company, because consumers gladly share their experience with others. It makes your popularity viral and creates new opportunities for growth and for targeting larger markets.

- ✓ *This produces better incomes;* a good digital marketing campaign is likely to help your company as far as higher incomes are concerned. è è Small and medium-sized businesses are highly advantaged by digital marketing strategies, as a 3.3-times better chance for faster and more efficient growth in sales.
- ✓ *This delivers better returns on investments*, which means better returns on investment than typical commercial channels are achievable by enhancing the sales and branding. Digital marketing is easy to monitor and track and calculate the performance as long as the intended action is taken by your targeted audience, for example by sharing contact information, subscribing or buying anything.

A steady traffic flow that turns into leads is the key to successful digital marketing. The more your company produces this sort of traffic, the more easily your return on investment can be realized.

If there are many visits to your website who don't turn them, this will eventually stop being there. Digital marketing is therefore important because it includes a variety of strategies and tactics that draw targeted traffic and achieve the desired results. Digital marketing works at the right people to get the right results. It guarantees the company's sustainability.

Digital Marketing Trends for 2020 you Should Know

Each year, advertisers are aware of developments to respond quickly to emerging technologies and remain ahead of the market. Technology patterns are evolving every year. It allows you to achieve a competitive edge and develop new ways of increasing your business, developing feedback and bettering ties with your existing customers.

In 2019, the year of growing rise in fact, video content, voice search and influencer marketing was focused on patterns in digital marketing last year... And you might wonder: "What will this year have for me? And now that 2020 is here."This is the digital marketing patterns you should take advantage of to boost your marketing strategy and reach a desired outcome in order to find the path you are going to take by 2020.

1. Voice Search

There is no question that voice search is growing more popular. In 2021, according to analysts, 50% of all inquiries will be voice-based.

Two forms of voice search are primarily available: those introduced by intelligent speakers such as Amazon's Alexa, Apple Homepod, Google Home and Microsoft's Cortana which provide immediate answer to your questions through search engines; and those installed on desktops and smartphones such as Siri and Google Assistants, which show search results in writing.

Top brands find improving on their voices because they are cost-effective and more efficient than ever before while more people use voice search to connect with these brands.

Businesses should also focus on using enhancement of speech engines. To create content accordingly, advertisers should use a more natural language SEO. It allows them to worry about what they can use in their voice questions and to concentrate on keywords that are long-distance, because searchers are likely to be more precise in the query. In a single question, for example, a shopper may inquire about time, size, place and other information, which are very important in order to allow written searches.

As a result, advertisers can use these incentives to deliver more click-through results for more tailored, specific content.

2. Smarter Chat

In recent years the number of chatbots is growing and continues in 2020. According to Report, 45% of end users would favor chatbots in customer service as a significant way of communicating.

Chatbots play an important role in improving the customer experience and helping advertisers to interact more with their customers-without doing much whatsoever. To order to understand the real problem to real time, they provide customer support through committed guidance and constructive communications.

For example, a web site user is approached by chatbot, asked for help or for more product information.

If the first choice is picked, a person will be contacted for assistance and if the next alternative is chosen, a series of automatic questions will be requested or forwarded to his forum or FAQ tab.

The growing trend is Whatsapp Business Messaging that according to Statista has become one of the world's most used messaging apps. However, it is not limited to personal use; businesses use the program for their daily activities on a daily basis.

In 2021 the traffic in communications should double. The main reasons for this go from 31 trillion texting in 2014 to more than 100 trillion in 2021, which is the largest digital Over - The-Top or OTT apps.

3. Micro-Moments

As more people use their smartphones to monitor their online activities, advertisers tend to use micro-moments to draw attention to themselves and make immediate choices.

When a buyer shops for something, checks for a nearby shop, wants to finish a job or buy, salespeople can use these kinds of micro-moments to generate tailored products and advertising.

To effectively leverage micro-moments, advertisers should consider each other's simple behaviors. Consider the "I-want-to-go moments" for example. Through taking up the "close me" searches that were 2x between 2016 and 2017 according to Google, Brick and Mortar stores will take full advantage of such a moment. It ensures the storage positions on their pages or devices are optimised. To order to increase your exposure to Search Engines to meet the client at the appropriate time, they can also go beyond that by generating advertisements for your shops or popular products.

4. Augmented and Virtual Reality Marketing

Augmented reality ads is one of the major applications that are now used by some marketers. It is the way to create a more realistic experience of stagnant or impossible situations that would include the' offering' as part of the buyer's' reality.'

In comparison to AR advertising, other businesses have used content for the purpose of increasing brand awareness through increased and augmented reality.

Of example, L'Oreal and IKEA have been willing, by visualising their goods before consuming them, to enhance their perception with their customers with virtual reality. Nivea, Starbucks and Volkswagen are other examples of large brands that have been active in growing reality.

5. Live Videos-More Stories

Live content is the fastest growing category of Internet video traffic due to the phenomenal waves in the last two years thanks to Twitter, Snapchat and Youtube.

Live Streaming Content is reliable, since it is free, takes a little while to create while it provides consumers with a real-time commitment.

It also has the potential, particularly if you want to add them to your blogs, to create greater impressions as newsfeed posts.

Live streaming content helps advertisers to connect as quickly as possible with their leads, improve relations with vendors, attract a wider audience, and increase the volume on their social networks.

6. AI and machine learning

This phenomenon doesn't go away shortly, with world leaders like Amazon, Microsoft and Google expanding their AI and machine learning capabilities.

AI helps advertisers to predict their consumers ' potential possible preferences on the basis of data collected. This knowledge helps advertisers to decide how they can better communicate with interested customers through different channels, like direct mail, sales or digital advertising.

Many sectors have started to use AI, including food and beverage, ecommerce, life science and healthcare.

Most grocery stores, for example, use big data to determine their goods best delivery times. Data from various sources such as wind, road transport and temperature can be obtained. Big data can also help to determine the effects on food quality of all these variables.

86 percent of consumers in the e-commerce industry say personalization plays a major role in their buying decisions. Ecommerce firms use the big data to avoid the profile and behaviour of their consumers so that they can construct a more personalized experience including tailored discounts or e-mailsfor re-engagements.

Researchers estimate that in 2019, AI and computer education will enter different new fields that concern occupations such as commerce, finance, accounting and even the spirit of academics like teaching.

7. E-Mail marketing based on commitment

As e-mail marketing gets smarter, advertisers are starting to be more cautious with delivering e-mails to customers participating on their lists. Of example, if a contact is closely related to your e-mails, you should be constantly updated about your company's material and promotions before it becomes a reliable customer. Nevertheless, if a recipient does not receive an e-mail for a certain duration, it is called a dead communication and will not accept any e-mails anymore.

Yet advertisers need to recognize all their leading habits to send the right email to the right audience. If the systems they use have limitations on their behavior-based grouping of their users into different segments, they should combine their apps with other software that require them to do that. After all the data determinations and the development of different segments according to specified parameters, advertisers can more effectively concentrate on their findings through behavioral emails.

For a customized view of commitment-based e-mails to improve, another clear path is reappearing: plain text e-mails.

It delivers these commitment-based communications to the intended customer in a more private and manual manner, giving the shared element a tailored dimension. In addition, since e-mails in HTML style featuring comprehensive graphics will increase spam capacity, advertisers view plain text as alternative ways of mitigating this issue. In fact, plain text e-mails address the user's need and improve the contribution rate.

8. Rich Lead Profiling

Information enrichment is growing increasingly important for businesses who capture and handle complex data for millions of organizations and companies. Marketers use data mining to share more information about their advice and personalize their strategy to reach them. The big advantage of enriching data is that it excludes all false or incorrect information about a particular activity such as the name, telephone number or street address that businesses have.

Those results are then used to get other data that is incomplete. Of eg, if you have an e-mail of a certain route, your name, telephone number, street address, your work and household condition will be included.

The last step is the process of optimisation. Such data are used to create useful observations with the different data analysis tools available. Marketers will draw practical results and give each of their manuals, an email to discuss his desires in particular, which in effect improves his ability to convert him throughout the funnel.

9. Push Notifications Browser

Push Notifications push into the web browser application field and are one of the world's most popular trends for 2019 growth. Organizations use tab pressing alerts to more efficiently meet their leads and communicate more effectively with their customers. The maintenance of consumers and increases in conversion rates are another major role for such alerts. Of example, ecommerce firms are using a button push to re-target their customers who have fallen off their carts to inspire them to buy.

10. Content personalization

The need for a tailored approach to content is more important than ever because it does not suit everybody and consumers want more importance. Although it is difficult to deliver the correct content at the right time to the right audience, it adds great importance to your content marketing campaign, since it plays an important role in improving the customer retention level.

Customizing or personalizing user information depends on visitor data to provide the appropriate content. This involves showcasing interactive landing pages based on specific parameters such as regional, demographic and behavioural assets and highly focused requests for interventions to be more successfully transformed.

To order to provide reliable, geo-controlled offers, Group on demands guests to verificate their position until their presence is on site.

In the e-commerce sector, product advertising has a good impact on customers, with 44% of users with customized shopping experience expected to be frequent buyers according to e-consultancy. While the phenomenon is common in recent years, in 2019 it is predicted that the magnitude of this trend will grow to more than $400B by 2021.

Effective Digital Marketing Tactics and Strategies in 2020 and Beyond

Through digital marketing campaigns, you will create a long scroll of all today's available technology or applications. While you'll probably hear several recommendations that all or any digital marketing tactics are the most important ones?

You need to concentrate on certain areas in order to succeed in the overly competitive global world of 2020. Although you may have read about these, how many specifics do you really know to make them effective? For this year and the next decade, they're all the same.

Look at everybody and see how much you do. Then decide which components you have to add. All of which range from SEO to landing pages. Elsewhere, you will learn some new stuff about local search marketing and the increasingly popular video format.

1. SEO

Digital marketing is nothing more critical than SEO, which in its continued nature could still be mystifying to you. Although it may still be daunting to Google's algorithms, you can better understand how it works if you work better with the definition.

If you want to excel truly, you should always have a professional to handle SEO for you. You would want someone who has worked on it for a while, while studying the fundamentals, to help you to fully realize the best strategies.

New HTTPS standards have already influenced SEO results, one of the most current tactics. Google also recommends that you migrate to HTTPS format if you are using HTTP pages. Most ways of communication that use HTTP pages are not considered safe enough.

Now that Google will mark these "non-secure," changing the HTTPS status of your website is important. Then it may become a fresh scarlet post on your search engine to be given a "non-secure" stamp on your website.

2. Search engine marketing

You can usually see it abbreviated as SEM if you are new to search engine marketing. You increasing the SERPs by way of paid advertising tactics in an internet marketing system.

You will also want a professional, particularly one with Google Ads and search / display ads, to support you in this area. For Google Ads, you will want to know how the process works first.

What you most enjoy is that Google makes their personalized Google Ads easy to use. You can choose between graphical display advertisements, YouTube video notifications and text-based search ads, or smartphone in-app advertising. All these will rely on your business style and your intended consumers.

With localized ad capabilities, Google makes it even easier to monitor the role of your ads, plus superior metrics Don't ignore other paid ads, Facebook advertising in particular. The latter helps you to conform to several ad formats.

3. Local Search Marketing

In recent years, you have seen a great deal of attention paid to local search marketing. In the next decade it will continue to be significant, as local companies realize the value that local customers will discover.

You can again use more Google contributions to continue with local search marketing. For Google My Company, the second one who searches Google based on the user's keywords will turn up your page. This includes your Google Maps service.

Google makes upgrading the listing simple, so that nothing is obsolete. Do not forget how important your social status and the value of online review are.

You will encourage users to post positive feedback on websites such as Yelp. You can use inbound marketing across social networks, start conversations and share relevant content. Inbound strategies draw you instead of competing for clients.

4. Content Marketing

Content Marketing is an important element for targeting the target audience as a connective relation to inbound marketing above. What is important with content marketing is to make the content meaningful, relevant and trustworthy in order to make it useful for people who consume it.

In the present time, you will focus on creating content that can relieve suffering and stay evergreen. SEO strategies like shortcuts or black hat only to switch to top search engines will not succeed because of the all-seeing eye of Google.

Hold happy as a leader, as many people would like to claim. You need to concentrate on web apps, native advertising, seo and marketing automation in order for content marketing to work effectively.

Take internet apps positively as 50 per cent of worldwide users now make up smartphones. Online ads will be influenced and the direction impact the brand is marketed. Automation systems deliver content at the right time to prospects on their mobile devices.

5. Remarketing

If they don't first respond to your site's banner ads, another important part of digital marketing will be prospects again. It works by monitoring such visitors and creating new advertisements and cookies on related websites.

For fact, you can create new advertisements on your website to boost your prospects. The data you collect from your site visitors provides valuable knowledge to promote your ads.

In the end, remarketing helps you keep pace with experiences, boosts brand awareness, and increases sales. You can also win your rivals clients by helping to offset your expenses in creating new advertising.

6. Adequate web design

Mobile user service is now more or less the norm, and that will continue in the next decade. Mobile screens are one of the most important parts of digital marketing to make the platform adhere. The only way to do this is by referring to the web design.

You will immediately interact with all mobile screens by using flexible programming. More than one model, like tablets and expanded use of intelligent clock.

You will want a SEO specialist for another part of RWD while you are consulting with a Web designer. AMP is a new open source code which allows users to load mobile web pages faster.

Google takes blogs that use this precedent, and take it seriously. It is particularly useful for you to frequently add material to a publishing site or to update it on your blog.

7. Email Marketing

You certainly did some email marketing, but how successful is that at the right time in achieving your intended goals? Email marketing is already an excellent tool to produce more leads through any other marketing approach than possible. You can also increase the conversion and revenue level.

Email marketing is one of the most effective approaches if you already suffer from excess spending on digital marketing. It is optional, in some situations, because outsourced resources are used.

It is also one of the most versatile communication strategies, as you can blend it with other outlets. You should add icons for social sharing, and reward systems. Eventually, email marketing lets you shorten the sales times with compelling content.

8. Social Media Marketing

You have already shared content on social media. But, what can you do this year and next to make it more effective?

To order to capture the viewers of today, you can read a variety of items, including automation to publish your content. If you meet consumers in other timezones, using software like Hootsuite to prepare for postal services is immensely helpful.

If you can show your power, you will also curate other content. Do not be too proud to do so because your knowledge and reputation will be boosted by luster. We would also reciprocate, because you curate the contents of others.

However, don't hesitate to employ influencers in the social media channels to share material on your own.

9. Automated marketing

As you can see, in various digital marketing strategies marketing automation is an important element. Understanding more about this should in turn be a top priority since it is a worldwide standard for businesses.

Despite 91 percent of successful companies now claiming technology is very important to their future, you can see what marketing is like now and what it is like.

Try to find a CRM platform and optimized marketing automation to excel in this. These can fit well together because you already have knowledge about your CRM. The automatic integration of marketing material on your contact lists lets you combine all your ads in one location, instead of using different sources.

Automation is most important in keeping the content cohesive across all platforms so that brand misunderstanding is avoided.

10. Marketing influencer:

Did you consider how you can go about a digital marketing strategy without spending a fortune? While you can save money by email marketing, contacting influencers does the same.

Though you think it's all about hiring actors to employ influencers to promote the Brand online. A social media influential person doesn't always mean that he is a star. It can be just someone with multiple followers and a good record in product development.

Researchers say that you must first recognize the most important influencers that require a little work. You should scan for hashtags in sites such as Facebook to see what people say about your industry-related topics.

Reach such social media influencers and ask them whether they are willing to promote your brand. In exchange for free goods, some may recommend to do so. But most will call for a fee.

Make sure the results are tracked to ensure your ROI. Keep in mind that those with less followers can have as much impact as followers with 10 times more.

11. Video

There have been a more visual culture in the digital world over the last decade. Much of this comes in different forms, but it hasn't risen to the top.

We have now reached the point where more content consumers prefer video to any other visual medium. Much of this is from massive viewing of plages like Twitch. Recent statistics suggest 87 percent of all internet advertisers now use some kind of video content. Notwithstanding, without compelling content you post videos won't matter.

More personalized content has lately become a standard, or at least directly targeting viewers ' pain points.

The same goes for your company's human appearance. Successful video marketing could include showing your company behind the scenes or highlighting your brand's human side. This means that one big theme in content marketing is being considered: storytelling.

If you give the client a compelling story and show that you can overcome customer's pain points, you have a strategy that can't miss. Even if not in a sequence the videos should be kept as short as possible. The target areas are as brief as ever, and with a quick hook you will have to tell your story.

12. Revisit Your Landing Pages

When, as part of your digital marketing strategies, you already have a landing page built, you are confident who will return before you go? This is a problem that should be at the core of your digital marketing activities. Both marketing experts echo how effective inbound marketing is powered by the landingpage traffic.

Maybe it's not very appealing to your landing page right now. This is overcome (in part) by web design, including where you make an argument and ads. Nevertheless, it goes beyond what you put on your website. For PPC advertising (pay per click) you're going to invest for putting your website ads on internet networks.

The choice is the purchase of sponsorships or simple email campaigns with other businesses. In the latter case, it is a common strategy to put a connection which brings the reader to your landing page.

To avoid complications, make sure that one is included on the CTA webpage. Even a CTA at the end of the blog offers the material a connective string to enable a second visit. However, look out for the topics above and below the fold. Kissmetrics once noted that putting CTA depends on your landing page length. A shorter page means that the CTA should be put over the tab.

CHAPTER TWO

Using a Digital Marketing Strategy to Increase Marketing Impact

A digital marketing strategy is a set of guidelines that detail what companies want to do and how they can accomplish their goals. This provides guidance for companies in their efforts to make this happen effectively and efficiently.

Given the value of a digital marketing approach, an estimated 65% of advertisers report that there is no digital marketing strategy in their wider marketing platform and 47 percent state that, despite trying to use digital marketing strategies, they have no digital marketing strategy at all. This puts these organizations, when attempting to get a foothold in the new world, at an enormous disadvantage.

Digital marketing has become highly competitive in recent years. By the end of 2020 there will be more than 3 billion projected worldwide internet users. The internet has become a key tool for people, particularly consumer brands, to communicate. When transparency has grown, the amount of content produced has also risen tremendously. In the last two years alone, 90% of the world data are produced. With this countryside even more dynamic, marketers must have a clear approach that leads and allows them to expand online. Without this, they run the risk of obstructing their attempts by creating content in order to obtain value–a material that waste time in giving consumers or the company itself real benefit and is often seen by virtually everyone.

Creation of a digital marketing campaign Good online marketing campaigns should provide an explanation of what the company plans to do and how it will do it. It should allow marketers in every phase of the process to see their final results. The approach can be modified as the business grows and further defines the less effective and working strategies.

Phase 1: Specify the goals and expectations

Companies should first create a list of goals that their digital marketing campaign strives to achieve. These priorities should be precise and quantifiable. Of examples, businesses may discuss a percentage increase in their speech, a specific improvement in output over the years or a certain amount of sales they want to reach. It ensures that the companies will start to build a route in the right direction. With these priorities.

Determine how each component is calculated after the targets are outlined. Identify KPIs that indicate whether you have met the goals you have set or not. It is simple with StoryBuilder on the BrightEdge platform. A whole set of metrics, for example y / or efficiency, revenue and voice share, can be calculated on this aspect of the platform.

Phase 2: Figure out the buyer's customers and their customer trips

After the company knows exactly what its marketing efforts can do, it then determines exactly who it is trying to reach with its ads. Step 2: SEO techniques have much greater significance for a target audience than other, more traditional marketing methods. Rather than sending information to specific demographics, marketers must realize, and therefore be able to inspire them to discover their website and their company, precisely what their target customers want to hear.

Marketers will concentrate on looking both at current market trends and their own consumers to better understand the potential people that the company wants to reach. You will look for patterns and developments that allow possible customers to be clustered into 3-5 main categories. Such classes give you insight into each group's pain points and goals and direct your marketing strategy.

Take the purchaser men, map them on the purchaser's ride. Use your perception of what these people want to see from you and build a contour of the types of content that will inspire you at every step of the journey. Remember that various content styles always fit best for people in various phases. Of example, blog posts may be fantastic at the beginning of the trip of drawing new audiences, while case studies and white papers are better suited for people in the centre. Comparisons that discuss the benefits of working with you throughout the match benefit those who plan to move.

Phase 3: Look at your current content

Now is the time to check your current content. Perform a fundamental analysis to figure out the products you already have and schedule it for the retailer trip for your different perfect clients. It allows you to consider how the content suits the pattern, where your weaknesses lie and where your digital marketing approach can be strengthened.

The figures for your existing content will also be studied closely. See which components are the strongest and separate explanations why. See how well the pieces are linked and whether they allow people to travel the purchaser.

Phase 4: Choose the material's keywords

The next significant step in your SEO approach will be keyword study. Keyword analysis needs to be separated from the old, dead SEO and keyword stuffing processes. Keyword research focuses on finding perspectives to recognize the subjects that are of greatest importance to your audience. You want to look at the words and subjects with the highest traffic results and build the material to address the audience's expectations and concerns.

You will carry out this work with the Data Cube, according to experts. To order to gain insight into what makes these pages rank and where you can improve and outdo them, you can take your analysis a step further by using the suggestion motor to look at the top 10 list.

Phase 5: Build, refine and deliver high value content

With your keyword analysis, customer data, journeys and insights into your most popular content, it's important now to build high-quality content which will attract your clients.

Such content should be guided by your understanding of your target customers and your established objectives. For instance, a greater interest in developing content for major publications or gaining followers on social media can include expressing the priorities of identity or brand awareness, which influence the effectiveness of your plan. Revenue-focused targets concentrate on the development and purchasing of content that leads customers throughout the entire consumer process.

This content must then be designed to help the search engines and users differentiate themselves. You should use the main keyword and a number of associated search-less secondary keywords. Sprinkle all text and title keywords, headings, meta description, URL and alt text with your keywords.

Once the material has been created, share it where the specific target for the product, such as social media platforms as part of your email list, can be found. A good following for the job encourages travel, engagement and backlinks.

Phase 6: Track your progress constantly

Understand that issues are always changing when you continue the transition to digital marketing strategies. Sometimes they must be adjusted to reflect exactly what does and doesn't work for a specific organization. Of example, you might find certain content pieces more popular or more successful. In the first step, tracking the KPIs you have developed will let you know how you are doing and how improvements are to be made.

SEO strategies and SEO guides are multi-step systems that need to look closely at what you are doing and what you are going to do. When specific online marketing techniques are designed and implemented, the ROI from your activities will become much more quickly measured and advanced.

Tips for Implementing A Solid Digital Marketing Strategy

If you own a business, you probably know now that you must have a decent digital marketing strategy to make the improvements you want to make in the new, global world of today. But where are you going to start applying a good digital marketing strategy?

✓ **Start with a simple and unified brand**

Before you go into the marketplace, the first step towards the full digital marketing campaign is taken. To continue, you need to establish a consistent and unified brand to enforce your messaging at every point of contact. It significantly improves client reminder and will keep the company in mind.

What's a name, however? A united brand is not just a slogan which incorporates both a visual identity and a plan to position a rival on a higher level. This not only benefits your clients, it also allows you to build a reputation before starting your digital marketing campaign, as you will always have a solid foundation to sustain your collateral.

✓ **The best SEO technique is to build a website**

How to get your website accessible online is SEO or Search Engine Improvements. The right SEO technique is absolutely essential to launch any digital marketing campaign in an environment where the online space is overcrowded to say the least.

SEO should always bear in mind when designing your company website. Whether you do it yourself or externalize the program, you will build an SEO person who understands what you have to do to show your sites. All the best practices will be recognized by Google and the other search engines by using the right keywords and creating good documentation to guarantee that your web is safe and stable. This will certainly increase the sustainable site traffic.

- ✓ **Use a range of different platforms**

The marketing strategy contains numerous outlets in the digital realm. The best thing about streaming is that these platforms can be tailored so that right people can see them every time. There is no lack of effective tools from programmatic and Google Ad campaigns to all available social media platforms. The key is to know which of these platforms will most often include the audience and bring your marketing budget into several of them.

Local companies can, for instance, choose to incorporate strategies created by keywords for their Google ads. The same organization can also build a location-based Facebook traffic plan. This kind of company would accept LinkedIn as a forum for recruiting, but it wouldn't influence people visiting their shops every day.

- ✓ **Do your homework when it comes to user experience**

But find that people don't float through the user process for you and make the sales you want to get through your digital marketing. The user experience or UX is a big technical dimension that people sometimes miss. This is so important to research properly or have someone who knows what they are doing applied.

UX can be incorporated into your websites, for example, by seamlessly and logically leading consumers from page to page. The way your customers interact with your ads, where they're led by tapping on a Social Media Connection and how they're going through your physical store can be seen throughout the consumer experience. There are several ways to introduce good user interface, large or small, and more account is taken of it, the more the consumers enjoy your business.

- ✓ **Building interaction material consistently**

You would think you should end it with all the advertisements in the right place and with the customer experience solidified, but it's not real. Any good digital marketing strategy has a plan in place to create content so that the platforms remain active and actively engaged.

It is one of the best things you can do in the digital strategy whether that means posting social media content to connect with fans on your website or producing written blog content for your site to promote SEO. Remember the saying–King's stuff.

Ways to Improve Your Digital Marketing Strategy

When new advertisers push into 2020, customers have become louder than ever before. Due to the mobile (thanks to the fact that more than 77% of adults have one), users will be everywhere at once. There are countless ways that customers communicate with brands online through social media platforms, software, blogs, etc.

This allows further opportunities for digital advertisers to communicate directly with such consumers. But there are more labels for every customer, who want to cut through the noise and genuinely crochet customers with enticing products.

With this changing climate, advertisers will constantly update and improve their digital marketing campaigns to ensure that noise is not blocked or missed. This is how advertisers should reassess digital marketing goals so that effects and outcomes can be maximized.

1. Conversion is not just leaders

Information is one of the main elements of an effective digital marketing campaign. That judgment and action taken by a marketing team will affect results and measurements. This means digitalizing in today's market intelligence, knowing where potential customers spend their time (which social platforms and websites).

Big Datacom and machine learning advancement has historically lead to more broad and effect conversion rates at an individual level while B2C marketing teams have preferred a massive platform and aim for better.

Marketing companies may move forward the buyer choice for purchasing by targeting specific categories of populations and markets with certain types of content, promotions or product recommendations.

2. Set the stage for a long-term return

Marketers should always take long-term interest into account when their strategic decisions when keeping it tentant to make short-term gains. To invest, advertisers would be smart to carry out due diligence and analysis in order to make sure the investment pays off in the long-term before spending resources on the one-off social media platform.

The same is true of devices and strategies. Marketers will ensure the solutions will help the team succeed in the long run and not just to fix the short-term problems while handling the purchasing process. It is not necessary that each aspect of a multi-annual project has been ironed out, but it is a good idea to have a growth plan and to consider how a method can help make the plan a reality.

Despite technologies evolving rapidly, the market will always have "now" and "hot air" innovations and developments. Marketers should be vigilant to consider the brand's competitive benefits when taking decisions that could have an impact on long-term growth or profits.

3. Customer service Double Down

Online advertisers should think of "What is customer service for me?"-experience with a brand has an effect on its view, but is sometimes easy to forget, so it is known as a' Customer Service.'" For digital businesses which have to replicate brand-conscious customer support strategies across several platforms and networks, this is even more relevant. This is a vital part of success in omnichannel marketing, which ensures that a single client has a smooth, streamlined buying experience, irrespective of the network or source.

Although customer service may be more relevant than online retailers to brick-and-mortar shops, many companies of today have shown the value of stellar service to e-commerce interactions. In creating the customer-centered image of the companies, digital advertisers play a major role. Whether customized e-mails, welcome pages or tailored product recommendations make this personal touch a big difference in consumers ' eyes. Apparently, a brand which knows them by name is 56percent more likely to purchase from customers. Consumers expect individualisation because they demand better customer support.

4. Create the final buying path

When advertisers can better understand their target base in greater detail, procedures can also be optimized and the definitive shopping pathway is established. Digital marketers can see precisely which content among users is most effective, and then strategically draw on it for optimum returns. If a company understands, for example, that a majority of customers come to its website from social networks, it can improve social marketing and develop dynamic workflows to bring the consumer from point A to B.

The last shopping trip is also to automate their shopping experiences online and smartphone. As online shopping trends and online shopping moves to mobile devices, marketers have to ensure that their pages are strong, that they are branded and that the shoppers can easily find what they are looking for. The smoother the shopping ride is, after all, the greater the chance.

5. Know when and how the procedures are refined

It is convenient for advertisers to really get their hands dirty when boasting about processing processes. It might be time to go back and re-evaluate where things went wrong if a system or procedure is just not working. This is also an excellent chance for A / B to test various campaigns and tactics. Marketing is a changing world and digital marketing is one of its most diverse features. Marketers will keep an eye on the metrics, details and where it may be necessary to improve. The systems are working.

Your digital marketing approach will change as the field of marketing evolves. It is important to be aware of the changing landscape and new technological advances that can ease the lives of digital marketers.

Reasons Why You Should Have a Digital Marketing Strategy

Any business trying to market itself online has an absolute digital marketing campaign–right? That's certainly the experience from reading the most digital marketing forums, which have for many years been eclipsed by the topic of how to develop a digital marketing plan.

Yet most companies are still not convinced on the table.

A research from Smart Insights, Digital Marketing Director, reveals that almost half of businesses have active and unknown digital marketing strategies. The other half is split between those with an individual digital strategy (17%) and those who have incorporated the approach into a generic marketing plan (34%). This would be the way that digital marketing has grown into' business as usual' for the more experienced marketers.

I am confident that many of the 49% of businesses who do not yet have a written strategy use digital media to achieve results, but have a builed digital marketing plan to improve partnerships with digital media including organic and paid advertising, retargeting advertisement and social media marketing.

Maybe they've got good excuses not to develop a plan.

Firms frequently advise me that their policies and proposals are already appropriate, and are rarely mentioned; that putting their agenda down in writing will trigger development and control issues; that new plans are not beneficial, because technologies and communication methods are evolving too quickly; they actually do not have the money or the time to build them.

Nonetheless, I am sure they would also profit from their strategy being written down.

The reasons for this are:

1. A written strategy gives you feedback and direction.

Organizations that have not outlined their approach may have a general understanding of what they want to do online and their organizational strategies.

You can know, for example, that you want to have more website visits, but can you tell how many? Maybe you want to attract more clients, but can you say which percentage or which networks are available? It is harder to know exactly what you need online and then to calculate how good you are without specific targets that depend on conversion funnel-based forecasts.

Creation of a written approach requires businesses to answer these key questions and devise a compelling plan for online interest, set the target audience specifically, and carefully consider all of the other building blocks for a successful digital project.

The obstacle with digital marketing is that you can focus on so many things that you can stretch too thinly or miss key events. You can choose to concentrate on key goal programs with a plan.

2. This means that everybody is on board–and on the same page

It is difficult to ensure that your digital business is broadly supported within the group. They can do this much better by having a written schedule that outlines what you are doing, how it blends into the other business goals of the Organization and how it tests whether or not it is successful. We have immediately a multimedia platform that can be marketed and protected, rather than just "some of us."

In fact, it means that everybody has to sign up for a dream and process. Each boss and managerwill easily, with no formal policy, formulate his or her own goals and objectives online and, all too often, everyone works for cross-cutting purposes without ever knowing it. Clarity is important! Clarity is essential!

3. You will find yourself more resourced

When you work without a plan, the complexity of your technology programme, and the training your team needs to perform, will be more difficult to develop in advance.

Sure, where and when the need happens you should ask for more money to hire staff, but always on your feet. If you could deliver a long-term strategy and personnel schedule, would it certainly be more effective–and simpler to do so?

4. It will restrict replication and waste

Even if you have adequate money, they can be lost without a strategy to make productive use of them.

Let's give an example of targeting. Most big businesses are going to engage in paid media by marketers to search and retarget, but sometimes they don't monitor the marketing budget enough to get the most out.

From my opinion, smaller companies often are more informed as they decrease the cost of digital media by identifying for example ad exclusions:

- ✓ Age groups that may not be appropriate for your company, e.g. young vs elderly
- ✓ Geographies including non-core markets
- ✓ Unfavorable keywords and labels on AdWords
- ✓ Rising spending in certain days and decline in other expenditure, i.e.
- ✓ Including, or excluding, prior customers or non-buyers and the use of lookalike or in-market budgetary targets Another case of duplication you can also see in bigger companies where different parts of the marketing department custom different equipment or tools or use a different way of using it.

In this scenario, a written approach is about better organization and there is a common set of knowledge and marketing tools to help the promotion of the lifecycle.

5. It will help you automate and stay ahead of schedule

Any website company has analytics, but many senior executives do not make sure their teams make or have the time to examine them. The adaptive approach will monitor the program to ensure continuous improvement.

You can also refine a plan. A strategy. A good strategy comparisons your market with rivals to show you where you are behind the curve and outlines explicitly which goals you need to accomplish online, helps you to evaluate what works and what isn't and make the necessary changes. Standard comments are included in the framework again, so that you have a report to respond to.

It doesn't have to be difficult to write a plan. Begin by outlining your objectives, strategies and KPIs for one to two pages. All you need to get going is a simple table which lines these up for each part of the marketing funnel.

Only this exercise would make a huge difference to your online success and you can later create a more full database. For help keep the process flexible, we recommend a 90-day preparation approach that does not only produce a report every year and then theoretically neglect the digital strategy. Alternatively, findings from the last quarter are checked every 90 days and key measures have been developed for the next quarter to help keep attention on them.

Fresh Aspects That One Should Know About Digital Marketing

In the last five years, marketing has shifted more than in the previous 50, from print to streaming. There are no signs of slowing down this rapid evolution. The SEO, social media, content marketing, paying advertising and email marketing are commonly used by advertisers for leading purposes. But over the last year there have been some dramatic changes in the digital marketing arena. Here are the new digital marketing trends that all advertisers need to learn.

1. Artificial Intelligence

Artificial Intelligence (AI) offers excellent digital marketing tools for the future. Some companies rely on the state-of - the-art capabilities of AI now, and many more continue gradually to incorporate AI for digital marketing. For starters, AI is used to simplify various activities by companies such as Uber, Microsoft, Pizza Hut, and others.

In almost every new software firm for 2020, AI technology, according to Researchers, will be widespread. AI is one of company's most important business prospects and is expected to grow global GDP by 14% by 2030. In other words, in the next few years industries that do not adapt quickly to artificial intelligence will be severely disadvantaged.

AI is able to examine consumer behavior, browsing habits and use social media data and blogging channels to help businesses better understand how customers find products and services.

2. Chatbots

In action, chatbots are an example of AI. Such interactive assistants are using instant notifications to communicate with consumers in real time. We also offer advantages including excellent service, meet customer expectations, automate repetitive processes and provide 24/7 responses. Mastercard recently created a bot for Facebook Messenger which decipheres what a customer wants and responds accordingly, using natural language processing software. Currently, chatbots are a crucial part of digital marketing in several studies. By 2020, 85% of customer service will be driven through chatboats. Innovation Enterprise reports. Businesses can save more than 8 billion dollars a year by 2022 with chatbots, according to the IBM.

3. Planning Buying and Publishing

Programming involves using AI for the purchase or selling of advertising space. This method dynamically collects, positions and optimizes the inventory of newspapers. The use of AI for automated purchasing of ads reduces the need for RFPs, human consultation and manual order implementation.

Programmatic advertising leads to greater change and lower purchase costs as it is faster and more efficient. The brand will adapt its message and build the goods for the right audience at the right time by means of programmatic ads. That way, a more detailed and customer marketing campaign can be accomplished with better efficiency. Real-time bidding is a well-known standard for system ads.

According to the researchers, about 86% of digital display ads are expected by 2020. In other words, the face of digital advertising evolves very rapidly.

4. Voice Search and Smart Speakers

Search Engine Land estimates that up to January 2019 there have been nearly one billion voice searches each month. According to ComScore, 50% of all searching were performed by speech in 2020; Voice shopping, according to OC&C Strategy Consultants, will rise from 2 billion dollars to 40 billion dollars by 2022. It is no wonder that companies reconsider their digital marketing approaches as voice search becomes increasingly common.

Currently, AI is smarter than it used to be and has contributed to mistakes of famous voice helpers like Alexa, Siri, and Google deteriorating. Researh says it's not only important to remain key to a Voice Search strategy. The goal is also to create a creative and personalized consumer experience, which will enhance brand loyalty and develop relationships.

5. Digital Marketing

Video marketing is probably one of the most significant marketing strategies. Research shows that 83% of advertisers agree that video provides them with a strong return on investment. Yet 52% of customers say they have made online purchases when they watch company ads.

Content marketing is now going beyond YouTube. Marketers also benefit from Video Advertising on Twitter, Snapchat and LinkedIn. Additionally, as the use of mobile devices is growing, users are more familiar with videos because they can provide the same details in any platform format.

6. Content marketing continues to prevail

The Google March 2019 algorithm supports revised and complete digital on a regular basis. Point Visible reports that 88 percent of B2B advertisers believe that advertising is a reliable and trustworthy platform for the public.

Marketers will therefore need to continue to invest in advertising, as Google puts emphasis on well-invested goods that are regularly updated. In other words, content marketing should continue to make a major contribution to the appeal and quantification of new customers for your website.

7. Omnichannel marketing

Omnichannel marketing offers the audience with a multichannel experience by using various platforms. It is critical, however, that brands deliver a clear, seamless message on every channel, online and offline. All marketing platforms have to be linked to one comprehensive strategy to achieve best results.

According to study, an omnichannel strategy leads to a 18.95% participation rate, a 250% higher level of sales and 90% greater retention of consumers. One field in which artificial intelligence lets advertisers perceive consumer behavior and create a more customized advertising campaign is another area.

Technology is changing how companies interact with customers, who become more informed and who demand an experience more personalized. You might need to invest in some futuristic technology in the immediate future to remain ahead of the curve.

CHAPTER THREE

When You Should Change Your Digital Marketing Strategy

Digital marketing is growing rapidly, which can sometimes sound alarming. Strategies that have worked in the past may not currently be successful. Would you know why many firms do not get their rivals ahead of them? It's just because they don't want to adapt to the changing digital media landscape. The great thing about a digital strategy, though, is that in reaction to real time feedback and performance estimates, you can change them on the move. Although it may seem impossible to adjust things too fast, you may not be able to find out if the strategy works for the long term. But if you wait long, your two valuable resources are likely to be wasted: time and money.

Having said that, how do you decide when your digital marketing plan is the right time? Here are 5 indicators that help you decide whether to interrupt your plan. That assist you with the fast-paced market.

1. Focusing on low-value metrics

If you rely on low-quality metrics such as prints and clicks, you can struggle to see your marketing exposure as impressions and clicks only let you know. And not the tactics ' real precision.

2. Just don't compromise on the public needs of your brand

Everybody wants to spread their brand name, but you don't want to overdo it by pasting the own. In reality, educate your content about the issues and needs of your audience. This would allow you to reach purchasers in the early days of the purchaser's journey.

3. Using keywords over time

While keywords must be included in your text, Google's focus still lies in supplying consumers with usability and web relevance. Google has nothing to do with how often the term "digital marketing plan" appears on your website 4. 4. Don't believe your instinct: obviously your previous experience is important. Yet it shouldn't just be focused on what has worked in the past. It's a bad idea as it could be completely irrelevant now what worked tomorrow. This will only help you achieve better results by driving your marketing strategy with objective data.

5. Not integrated: It is too normal for digital marketing campaigns to be done in silos, whether it is a veteran digital marketer, This firm or start-up. It's faster, but it's not effective, of course. It is accurate that when combined with traditional channels, the modern solution is better used.

Common Misconceptions About Digital Marketing

You will know how effective it has now become because you know what digital marketing is. Okay, beginners often face certain growing misunderstandings about digital marketing. Finally, in this competitive environment, they will suffer early loss. Believe it or not, other people have experienced the same circumstances as well. That is why; I believe I need to warn you what can mostly have negative consequences on your attempts to sell the digital media.

There is no question that digital media marketing has brought business development fresh impetus for faster growth in this technology-driven environment.

Nonetheless, some common errors a marketer can prevent are:

1. Higher time consumption combined with lower performance: Time against outcomes is the first thing that fooled a beginner. It is a reality that in the internet or web media arena there are hardly any shortcuts to profitability (except for pay / click advertising)! You will wait for results for some time before you begin promoting your business online.

Rework on strategy will lead to desired results after some testing. Nonetheless, you should not stop working on marketing ploys on digital media. You need to note or hand on the findings of digital marketing for a long time to your subordinates. As companies run, revenue collection is much easier than off-line marketing systems.

2. It is too technical and hard to track or measure: I would personally tell you that I have come across people who simply try to refute web or online marketing, as it is a bit technical. It is too complicated and difficult to monitor or quantify. Some of my friends and clients suggest, "You understand better things than you do the technical knowledge." And I can say that there are so many tools to monitor so measure the performance of your digital marketing activities as we think about the monitoring process. For starters, there are various keyword analysis tools to help you understand the best words or sentences that will allow you to lead and surpass your competitors ' search results in Google.

3. You need to invest lump sum money for success: One drawback that can really hinder an early start in the internet or web marketing arena is money. Another setback is money. Many people have a great misunderstanding that physical and internet marketing requires a substantial investment in your marketing budget. Actually, that's not true at all.

Whether or not you hire a digital marketing specialist, rather negligible commitment will begin to show you further outcomes. Better results from other traditional communication strategies can even be predicted. To achieve results in a first-hand way, multiple free methods are applied.

4. SEO must die so that this madness stops: There are so many Big Brothers that have built a deep knowledge of Google and SEO themselves. They are of the opinion-Google now cannot or must not stick to conventional methods for optimizing websites (meta tags, content and other information) so that the money does not need to be spent in digital marketing or online marketing (SEO definitely does). Other methods should be practiced.

These concepts are nothing more than misunderstandings about digital marketing! With Google and other search engines, the on-site SEO (work on Meta and content) still has value. Such measures lead searchers to catalog and display user requests the best results. Sure, SEO strategies are evolving to provide the consumers with the best results and will not die before search engines are available.

5. Social networking is internet or online marketing: In this age of Instagram, Twitter, "what's up" people are deeply underestimated. We began to believe that social media marketing is all about digital marketing. You do not have to do anything else if you can sell your company through social channels. But I must say to beginners, don't do the same! When you scan, there are so many other strategies that lead to results. Do not spend your time on social media marketing absolutely. Of example, to make your online presence easier for the most people, you have to know and work. And to do this, you will learn certain key strategies that are included in the marketing of digital media.

Amazing Benefits And Importance of Digital Marketing For Growth

The planet witnessed a paradigm shift from analog to digital over the last decade roughly. More and more consumers use all sorts of information digitally, and digital marketing becomes the best way to reach their clients. We wonder why it is relevant for digital marketing.

The value of digital marketing is not only for the benefit of advertisers, but also for users. Let us look at the value of digital marketing and grasp it.

1. Better Growth Options for Small Businesses

Digital marketing is essential for your business in selecting your marketing strategy as per your budget and to meet a wider public at a lower price. Even a decade ago, it was a challenge for a small business in particular to sell a product. They had to use humble strategies with almost negligible promises of effectiveness.

2. Better conversion rate

Companies which opt for digital marketing may calculate the conversion rate by means of a simple method in real time. This shows the proportion of audiences who become guides and eventually customers, and ultimately buy the product or service. SEO, social media marketing and email marketing are the ways to deliver a fast and effective channel of communication to the customer.

Surprisingly all the traffic you can get on your web is not fruitful, but digital marketing just helps you to reach people who need that type of service and therefore offer better transfers.

3. Create brand reputation:

To create an impeccable image for any company that really needs to survive. It has become clear in recent years that consumers will always favor a business that has no related controversies. Digital marketing's value today lies in giving you many ways to develop a personal relationship with your clients.

4. Consumer Solving Problems

Whether it is email marketing or social media, you should give the consumer always solutions to their problems and link them with your company by live chat access. You can easily convert the website and social media account into a position where the user can ask questions, make suggestions and thus take a positive link with you.

5. Engagement To android clients

Almost all of the pages are now rendered in a manner that is easily visible on the mobile phone since Google's first web upgrade. This is because almost all consumers have access to a smartphone and most also try items on the same phone.

6. Trust in your market expansion

Your products and company are available on several channels, allowing customers to compare your offerings in line with their level of experience. The new ones are immediately converted by a constructive and beneficial adjustment by a satisfied customer. In effect, this creates a strong brand image in the eyes of new consumers that leads to more sales.

7. Good ROI of your Investment

The scenario is more inclusive today, whereas earlier budget budgets have been distributed separately to every advertisement sector. Even a low investment in an email marketing strategy has the potential to produce consumer commitment outcomes. The use of web analytics helps the company owners to learn if your website delivers outstanding returns.

8. Cost-effective digital marketing

A small business must save its money before it actually reaches the green zone and starts to prosper. Digital marketing gives you the opportunity to meet multiple consumers on your budget at the same time. You should design a marketing strategy to use only budgetary types. If there are budget constraints, the niche markets should always be focused.

9. Higher income potential

As the amount of money invested is less, the return on investment is much better. According to a new Google survey, digital marketing produces 2,8 times more sales compared to traditional approaches. This combined with the fact that here's a fast conversion rate to guarantee you mince money as soon as you get in the pool.

10. Computable method of marketing

The success of traditional marketing is very difficult to track, but every phase of progress is tangible with the use of digital marketing strategy. Digital marketing works in real time to show the effectiveness of each strategy. You will select the best strategies with the best results through this. You can then easily change the campaigns to make them effective.

11. Expanding public reach

Digital marketing gives the audience the most important benefits. Current marketing restricts you to certain locations and regions, based on the scope and size of your demographic and print media.

Your reach can be focused further on digital marketing. Your target is more likely to spend time on social media platforms such as Instagram, Youtube, etc. where you can share ads and connect more.

12. Easy Adapting of Tactics And Strategies

Another major advantage of online marketing is that they are very simple to understand. Easy to adapt tactics and strategies. Through way of strategies, you can easily understand which outcomes are produced and which are not accomplished. Online marketing tactics that provide you with real-time results.

You can easily share your blogs on various social media platforms, for example if you want to advertise your blog page. You will increase your interaction with your customers very quickly and accurately by way of content marketing.

13. Could Start With A Limited Budget As Well

Everyone has a budget problem and so many corporations have not supported themselves. Nonetheless, you benefit from digital marketing to support your company very smallly. Digital marketing helps small and medium-sized businesses with small investments.

The data are discussed below, according to Report, how digital marketing tools support different small businesses.

Of example, the online marketing can play an important role if you make handcrafted art, but you don't have resources to fund your company. A minimum of 10,000 people allow the content to be shared on social networks, which have a budget of 300 per day. This allows you particularly to advertise your company to your target audience for a span of one month.

14. Go beyond your borders

Digital marketing is very special in nature to support the business. You have to come out and make some change in your comfort zone. You can benefit from digital marketing if you take an active role. Digital marketing's job is very fast, since it incorporates SEO, SMO, SME and other processes.

Online marketing's outlook is actually very bright. But while marketers engaged earlier in the marketing strategy of each other, the emphasis has now turned to a battle against the internet as a whole. It is time for businesses to use various modes and forms to expand and affect consumers in action.

It is only possible to survive in such markets by designing and implementing a marketing strategy that shows its peculiarity and offers consumers a justification to choose from you.

Why Your Business Needs Digital Marketing Services

The culture has certainly changed over the last couple of decades. With the invention of computer and Internet, our lives have been completely transformed. Okay, for everything else you don't have to go anywhere. You can use the internet and with just a few taps you will do a lot. Thanks to the Internet, too, the relationship between businesses and brands with the target audience has changed immensely. Business owners can now support their brand and expand their scope only through good online marketing.

You certainly will find support from many companies offering digital marketing tools for business, if you don't really know all this.

It is fair to assume that you know about the power of the internet before going into the details. The point is that every day it will become bigger and wider. It is a simple fact that you should also get into the digital space to achieve better marketing results. Anyway, this is an insight into why internet marketing should be taken into account precisely for your company:

- ✓ **The growth of brand awareness**

Your brand awareness is among the most critical aspects of running a business. The more customers you get into the business, the more sales you will get. It's so simple. But, given today's heavy competition in the world of industry, better brand recognition could become quite complicated. But with digital marketing, you will drive the brand into the mainstream. Because there are no real restrictions on the internet, you can distribute the brand to almost everyone you can.

- ✓ **The Consumer Targeting Potential**

You target all kinds of people in the old-school marketing techniques with few of them involved in your company.

In reality, there is no easy way to target those who are in your company. Nevertheless, digital marketing, on the other hand, just helps you to reach and promote potential customers. You have a lot of analytical instruments to help you determine what kind of individuals your potential customers are and how they can be addressed. The most important aspect of increasing sales is meeting right consumers.

✓ Cost-effectiveness

The most important thing that you have to do is cut down expenses if you want to build an organization and develop it with steady revenues. There is no place for traditional marketing approaches to do so. But you can save a lot of money by cutting the cost of ads if you collect digital marketing for business. It is best to recruit and let the global markets do the job for you if you want to do this right, because they are aware of its ins and outs.

✓ Greater loyalty to customers

The fact that buyer engagement is among the most important aspects of business operations is evident. All comes within the radar when you advertise your company, respond to your questions, or receive feedback. The more you do this, the more the likelihood that your client returns.

You face various challenges to gain a great deal of consumer loyalty with offline marketing strategies. But if you want a multimedia approach, you can use a number of tools to connect even more with your clients. You can use various media such as email, video, photos, infograms and more to promote your process. Using live chat you can satisfy your questions. There is no limit to the possibilities.

✓ Time & Energy Saver

It is very important to manage your time properly when running a business. Besides, while using the resources to stop a burnout, you need to be conservatist. Feeling relaxed and stress-free will help you spring and walk.

You can save a lot of time and money online marketing. In reality, you should stop bothering about promotions and concentrate on the flawless operation of your business.

You should outsource to a marketing agency for a better position and access the digital marketing tools for the client. You can therefore focus solely on your business and let these guys do the marketing job for you.

Everybody's physically off. It is extremely important to have a digital presence for your organization in this age of information. If you want to boost your client presence and sales, consider adding enterprise digital marketing tools to your advertising plans. It is high time you took your business to the next level.

Tips to Start a Career in Digital Marketing

As the Internet is continually used by businesses to generate sales, there is no greater need for expertise in digital marketing. It is an industry that is rapidly evolving and has many challenges, but also many benefits, including probably competitive profits.

If you have been thinking of changing gears and becoming a digital marketing company, it is time. And happily, it is not mandatory for you to begin with a traditional marketing degree, although some preparation will help you get your foot at the door.

Here you can do to launch a digital marketing career right now:

1. Creating an online presence

Nowadays, you may not be there without an online presence when it comes to finding a career in almost any region. This is particularly true for digital marketing for obvious reasons: a prospective employer will first look online for applicants and, if they can not find you, will move on to the next person with a selected image.

Build your own digital marketing blog, your Social Media Accounts, your portfolios, etc. Tell them what you can really do.

2. Know the Latest Trends

Digital marketing is an evolving and ever changing profession, learn the latest trends. You will keep up with the latest developments if you choose it as a profession. This industry's demands vary over time and someone else is waiting for it to take its place if you fall behind. Attend immersive workshops, take classes online and do everything you can to stay ahead instead of just keeping up with the game.

3. Use your creativity

Digital marketing allows you to make a number of innovative donations. Yes, there are structured approaches and frameworks for some programs, but you can always build and create things with your own flair.

The imagination is focused on digital marketing, so if you have an idea that fits, try. The more imaginative you are, the more likely you're to find this dream job and win it.

4. Build a Good CV

Make sure you build a diverse resume that reveals how important your talents are before you start applying for jobs. You shouldn't restrict yourself to just one program, especially when working in a creative industry such as digital marketing.

Go online and look at specific CV models and tailor yours to digital marketing practitioners.

5. Get out of there and network

It is necessary, and the best way is through networking, to get your name out there. This not only reminds people of you, but also offers you great connections that can support you in your career in many ways. Another individual can know where specific training will take place. Some person could have a good job. You can also benefit from your experience and build a list of professionals that you can use for a great team.

6. Read about analytics

You need to consider analytics in order to know how effective your marketing campaigns are. The data shows how well a campaign is doing or how bad, and it lets you figure out how the next time you can improve things. You do not need to go to college for a degree, but many online classes help you learn how algorithms work and how to use them. You can also use your own time.

7. Get some practice

The only way you get a career is through training. Get some experience. You may have to do some casual work, but this is a good long-term investment. Use all the skills you learn, support your buddies or community organizations with projects, and work on all sorts of side jobs that provide a lot of experience before you decide to apply for digital marketing positions on a long-term basis.

8. Say "Yes" to anything

We have been touching on free work, and we can't stress enough how important it is to do everything to give your first digital marketing job the exposure you deserve. Take jobs that other internet advertisers do not want. Take free work. Prove that you can take on every project and make it your own and excel in every endeavor.

You won't just gain experience, but prove you're willing to work hard.

9. Achieve Trusted Certification

Without a college degree, anyone can become a Digital Marketer but those with a Digital Marketing certification are the applicants who get the best position. There are courses to take that will help you train for the qualification exams, and you should get accredited sooner rather than later if you really are thinking about digital marketing as a profession.

This will make you stand out in a crowd of seasoned but not qualified digital marketers.

10. Be prepared for entry-level jobs

Nobody will start at the top of their careers irrespective of their qualifications, skills and experience. You may not get the position that you want instantly, but if you wait for it you will get there. You'll probably start as a juniors digital marketer, or as an intern, until you can show that you can handle more roles and are willing to work hard to make your job a success.

The Top Digital Marketing Trends That Are Transforming Businesses

The media business has been stormy with digital marketing. It has become an important marketing tool for encouraging and providing attention to the goals of your brand. With innovation in the areas of social networks, internet media and user experience continuously being witnessed, the reach of digital marketing is growing in height. We have taken up the leading developments in digital advertising to help companies stay aware of such prospects and to enable them to meet successful online goals.

✓ **Video streaming live**

Live video streaming has gained a lot in 2016 and is growing rapidly in current times as well. A marketer can communicate with consumers and is an effective tool. Video streaming services like Facebook Live and Periscope, which help users rationalize real-time content to get updates through social media, gained momentum from live video sharing. This pattern is very popular and will possibly continue for a long time in the digital marketing space.

✓ Unique content still rules the digital space

All digital advertisers believe that the' king' in the online world and this future development are special and high-quality material. When the content is distinguished by creativity and consistency, it means that the reader is fully involved and inspired.

✓ Social influencers are crucial assets for your business

Social influencers play an extremely important role in creating a loyal trail and knowledge of your brand: social influencers and existing Bloggers play a crucial role. It is not easy to reach the target audience as new social media channels are launched from time to time. Influencers and writers, though, share a committed dedication to catching and engaging the audience. Choosing the right people to promote your product can thus help you reach your target group and therefore make your company flourish.

✓ Users are glued on their mobile phones

The way a customer connects and shares information with the world by providing access to critical apps and social media platforms has been revolutionized by smart phones. Our daily companions have become mobile phones and ipads. Their dependence continues to increase. It is critical that the merchants take this reality into account and those who do not.

✓ The next big thing is increased reality

Pokemon Go's huge popularity gives the advertisers an indication that experiments with increased reality can last a very long time. Today, consumers are keen to encounter these concepts of increased realism which mean that marketers have plenty of potential gains. Get set to see further developments relevant to AR in the coming years.

How To Build A Career With Digital Marketing Lead Generation Techniques

Everybody is already aware of the importance of internet or digital marketing. It can be difficult to generate online sales without the aid of digital marketing. We usually mean lead generation when we think about digital marketing. It is the main aim of online commercialization; the more you have, the better the sales number in your product. If your blog doesn't get enough views, it can't deliver the results that it wants to produce. This is why organizations spend a great deal of money attracting digital marketing talent and it will definitely be the best time if you want to have a job in this field.

You must be aware of the strategies mentioned below to produce leads for a client. Such strategies have always been quite successful in increasing the rate of visits to any website, which also increases the sales figure in turn.

Let us illustrate to you, then, how these techniques work in lead generation.

1. Search Engine Optimization

We heard a lot already. SEO aims at improving the website in compliance with different search engine laws or guidelines. Yet we say mostly Google, though. Every day internet users around the world perform millions of digital searches. It is quite clear that the second page of the search result is hardly accessible to most people.

SEO tactics can therefore boost the site's rating and allow it to pick up a search result on the first column, which will in turn lead the company forward. Regardless of whether your business was inherent in B2B or B2C, SEO may both boost your website's visibility. Yes, SEO accounts for 40% to 60% of the overall lead production for the majority of businesses.

2. PPC

A lot of people seem to underestimate the importance of this strategy when learning about pay per click campaigns or ads. But you will learn why it is so important if you look more deeply into it. The worth of the paths produced by this approach is very high and most of the pathways are safe shot sales. Google AdWords certainly control the world in this strategy, with alternatives such as bing marketing, Instagram, Twitter etc.

3. LinkedIn Marketing

The approaches from LinkedIn Pro are particularly useful when it comes to creating recommendations for B2B clients. Already, more than 400 million users of LinkedIn. This is a huge platform for businesses that search for consumers. One of the main approaches involved in this case is profile optimization.

When an effective profile is available, it is time for a productive community to be created. As a digital marketing specialist, you certainly need to focus on building a powerful group that can create leadership. It is easier to find potential clients if you have a large group at LinkedIn Pro.

4. Social Media marketing

It is highly important to keep up with different social media channels such as Facebook, Twitter, Google+, Pinterest, LinkedIn, and Ozone at this period. According to some studies, almost 50% of Facebook users and over 65% of Twitter users are motivated by their feedback while researching on the purchase of an item. Therefore, you must remain active on these social networking sites if you want to reach a large number of potential customers of your company.

You will consider how to attract followers on Facebook, Twitter, Google+ and many other sites as a Social Media Marketing practitioners. This is one of the easiest ways to connect. It is also important to keep the attention of fans, who can regularly post or upload relevant and interesting content, whether text or image / video.

5. Detailed nature of your landing page

Landing page directs an internet customer or web page client to the sales page of your company. Different types of landing pages that exist, including Facebook ads, Pay Per Click ads, Twitter ads, direct mail, etc. Therefore, if you can design highly efficient landing pages for your customer, they definitely help to create a good number of instructions for your customer.

A destination page and its contents are sufficiently enticing to force users to bait. The online users will find the sales unwavering and at the same time trustworthy. You can get more possible clients for your products in this manner.

6. Affiliate marketing

Affiliate ads represent the advertisement that offers affiliates the incentive and allows them to attract company guests or clients. To people who do not know the reward. It is therefore a way to outsource the business ' marketing component to the affiliates and thus increase the overall efficacy of the Marketing Program for your client.

As a digital marketing specialist, your task should be to create a good strategy for your customers ' affiliate ads. In this situation, it is also necessary to create affiliate links. You should pay enough for your customer's affiliate marketing plan. More and more leads can be obtained through this way.

7. Tech Forum Discussion

Debates are always fine, and regional limitations no longer apply as they take place on the online platform. More people can join the forum to express their views or facts. The online discussion forums can be very useful for digital marketing specialists in this respect.

You can use the forums to cleverly position information so that more users can be drawn to your website by the material. The internet fora must be chosen carefully, though, because there are not many participants or guests to all the fora.

8. Regional Listing and white labels

We all know of the regional directories that are used to access the service provider contact information. You can also find such directories in the online world, and such a local listing can be used to get more information for your business. Nevertheless, you have to ensure that the connections are from white labels on the local list.

9. Blogging & posting content

Blogging is something that everyone knows about, and it can be a good way of creating leads. The online users also search blogs and visual contents for details and can provide you with the necessary information through the combination of marketing elements.

Many blogging platforms, for example, only require the web users to enter content after some easy steps, such as as requests for user contact details; asks the user to click on a link, etc. You can also educate online users on appropriate and insightful newsletters. You can also sell other products discounts.

10. Email Marketing

This is one of the best ways for businesses to get more business customers. Email marketing software is available, and hundreds of potential customers can be reached every day with their support. E-mail marketing involves contacting people, but in large quantities via firing e-mails. According to some research, you can get up to $40 in exchange for every dollar spent on email marketing. It's a very nice sort of investment, then, definitely.

You have to understand the various aspects of the E-Mail Marketing campaign as a specialist in digital marketing. You can provide more information to your client by choosing the correct application for email marketing. You will keep customers up to date on new offers from your company via email marketing, and this will in effect allow them to visit their website.

That was some of the leading strategies that you can use as a digital marketing specialist. Such methods can be applied in many directions and become an authority in these systems. It would be better to ensure the prestige and the importance of the digital marketing course before taking every test. You also need to learn these methods effectively before using them for the website of your clients. So spend some time with these strategies to learn more about them. You will definitely be well ahead of you.

CHAPTER FOUR

Costly Digital Marketing Mistakes to Avoid in 2020

Marketers are working on and introducing their Digital Marketing Plan 2020 with the new year here. All experts plan to expand their business, develop their brand and be a pioneer in their industry. Although it is important for a sense of urgency to accomplish all those targets, errors are to be avoided during the preparation and implementation processes. Such mistakes will reverse the company's goals, contributing to lost time, effort and cost.

1. NOT Aware of your demographic

Your digital marketing approach starts with a first place to know your customers. Your entire plan will fail without a clear understanding of your market and its desires. It is not only about posting news, tweets, and Facebook posts but digital marketing is about making a profit for your efforts. You will not be compensated for the performance you are expecting if you don't consider your target well.

2. LACK OF FOCUS

There must be a clear focus beyond understanding the target. You know what works first for fast, quality improvements in the places where you spend. Long-term milestones are part of your digital strategy, but strong incentives along the way contribute to a continuous effort to achieve faster targets that maintains the entire organisation's energy.

3. Try SET THE RIGHT EXPECTATION

Aspirations are crucial to the success of your marketing staff and the awareness of where the company can meet its annual goals. Set a realistic target with each campaign started. The budget for the initiative and the way you approach the right audience can be variables to determine the goal. Study previous campaigns to analyze the results and factors involved in them. Similar figures and categories of markets are discussed. To know or predict the timeframe between schedule and success is also a major factor in determining what outcomes are to be achieved.

4. LACK OF METRICS

Performance assessments are an essential part of any campaign strategy. Test outcomes from your campaigns against those metrics to assess where you get the best returns so that you can spend in future campaigns intelligently.

5. NOT Virtual USING in the most efficient way

Do not post to a virtual forum only for the sake of it; use the site for your benefit. Know the strengths of each platform for your business. For consumers, Twitter can be the best platform and LinkedIn can be the best tool to promote purchases. Conceive the campaigns through the web to obtain the best results.

6. NOT ENOUGH CONTENT

Like social, content is essential but needs to be strategic. Publish content that's:

- ✓ Relevant to your brand
- ✓ Speaks to the value of your product(s)
- ✓ Connects with your target audience and presents a solution for the problem(s) your business solves.

7. EVOLVING WITH YOUR AUDIENCE

It relates to your opportunities and clients. Determine what is best addressed by your audience: what led to the most positive engagement? You may have to make minor or significant changes in your digital strategy on the basis of your review.

8. NOT DETERMINED BUDGET

Budget is a major factor in the success of a campaign, especially when you start social campaigns. Learn your budget so that your team can set realistic priorities and goals.

9. So INFORMATE

The field of digital marketing continues to evolve and is aware of best practices, trends and what people seek allows businesses to maintain their position. Do not stop learning how the company can be improved with digital marketing resources.

10. LACK OF PLANNING

The most serious mistake in executing a digital marketing plan could be due to a lack of planning. Your digital strategy will represent your identity, identify your market, and specifically prioritize your business development.

key factors that make digital marketing plan successful

Sometimes, only a few differences exist between effective Internet marketing tactics and promotions which do not achieve their objectives. Nevertheless, the secret between overwhelming success and absolute failure is these small differences.

You have to learn the ingredients in the recipe for success if you want to make your digital marketing plan work. These are some of the main factors that make every digital marketing strategy a success:

1. Through digital marketing, how do I succeed?

Your company may have an infinite marketing campaign budget, but it should not allow you to disregard ROI. In calculating the ROI for the use of tactics, even mainstream advertisers are quite unexpectedly lax.

Marketers then calculate their preferences and shares popularity. These aren't therefore useful indicators to explain how much you spend on a digital marketing campaign in return for money.

The marketing team needs to understand ROI really well. This is perhaps the most important tool to consider without bias which strategies work best for your company.

2. How do you execute a successful campaign?

If the digital marketing strategy for your business does not have any targets, it operates like a speed car with no pilot, which ultimately fails and explodes. A digital marketing strategy, like everything else, should have a simple set of goals.

For instance, if the marketing team wants to attract ten thousand new Facebook profile page, this is the target. It's important to track it once you've established such a marketing target. If not, months or even years may take to reach a target. The marketing team can also consider where the campaign is going by keeping track of the goals. In the middle of a campaign, adjustment of courses is also much simpler because long-term targets are established.

3. Exhaustive data analysis

Businesses like to collect data such as children collect Halloween candy. Everybody plays in the data collection challenge, but only a few know what to do after data collection. A vast amount of data on the target audience of the product, brand awareness metrics, etc. have little use without proper analysis. Recruiting a professional independent copywriter specialist will help you determine how your business can boost its online marketing campaign.

That's right; the evidence the marketing team has obtained must be carefully analyzed. Now it takes time and tremendous mathematical knowledge to analyze the data. This is why most organizations do not evaluate the data they collect.

But don't let the plan be statistical. Recruit or persuade the internal research department of third party consultants to be informative about the data collected. It needs to be done several times a year on a regular basis.

4. How do I use digital marketing video content?

Do not underestimate the video's strength. Video content consumption has increased in recent years, particularly as smartphone use has grown. Consumers prefer film, and this medium is used throughout all stages of promotion and shopping.

Image is versatile, too. Advertisers may simply create text articles and video-based information to use popular content and highlight further. Image also spreads through different platforms such as the internet, social media, mobile devices and Television. This is the strength of content that can be gained from the digital marketing strategy.

5. For digital marketing is email marketing still important?

When it comes to customer service, there is one major error by companies: informing people about social media posts and comments online.

Given what you might have read, social media is not the best way to reach consumers with your content. In the long newsfeeds that are always refreshed with new material, the videos will easily be lost.

The easiest way to obtain the material is by e-mail to consumers. To order to reach the most loyal customers, the digital marketing campaign must have a good email service schedule.

E-mail is personal and is currently the best way to meet the right client for the right kind of content. You can use a lot of free online marketing resources to create an amazing email marketing system for your small business.

6. How do I select the right online marketing channels?

In digital marketing, more is not always better. The more focused the plan is, the more effective it will be. Therefore, do not use any single available platform to waste your money.

Choose the right channels for your business. A qualified SEO specialist will help you determine the right ways to grow your brand, review your past results and plan ahead. Data analysis and tracking of ROI will help the marketing team identify the best results for the campaign.

7. What is relevant for digital marketing to our customer feedback?

It might be easy, but most advertisers disregard the input from polls, internet polling and consumer reviews. User-generated data provides a wealth of information on the facets of an operating company and the factors that turn customers away. Don't depend on expert advice absolutely.

The regular customers in your business are those who can tell you what succeeds and what doesn't. Pay attention to your consumer reviews to better understand how your online marketing strategies can be enhanced. Bring into your digital marketing campaign the lessons you draw from feedback.

The world of digital marketing continues to change. Therefore, companies are well familiar with the strategies they use in order that brand recognition is generated and sales are improved. Yet corporations ought not to remain long lost. The businesses who master digital marketing's complex language will be the ones who will stay ahead.

Reasons How a Digital Marketing Program Can Help You

Industry experts agree that digital marketing can change industry and consumer experience entirely in the future. Corporations are looking to develop comprehensive digital marketing campaigns. Digital marketing will open up new career opportunities due to its scale.

It would therefore be a good career decision to apply for an accredited digital marketing course. Let's look at how you can benefit from a digital marketing plan.

1. Wide range of career opportunities

Digital marketing provides a great career scope! You should pick the one that fits your style. The areas to choose from include: satellite communications, copywriting, research, e-commerce, PPC, e-mail marketing, internet marketing, social media, web developer and web designer, etc. 2. Competitive pay packages: As competition for digital marketers is growing, a higher compensation offer can be negotiated. The more you can expect the better the expertise you have.

2. Boost the business

Digital marketing is a lifeline for young, small and existing companies with the majority of customers online. You can learn how to develop an internet customer base by taking a digital marketing course. It also helps you to increase your investment distance.

4. Become a Freelancer

If you want to give way to a freelancer job or continue your new career as a consultant, a digital marketing platform is the right way to go. Such courses are often offered online and in a number of modules. Therefore, according to your time, comfort and learning intensity, you should change the course.

5. Up Skill, Re Skill or Cross Skill

You could be a conventional marketing boss more wants to know new media. You could be a president. You might be a web developer who wants to update your current skills. Perhaps, you could be an HR director who would like to turn to digital marketing. In any case, you can use digital marketing programs. Ironically, you will advance or change it through every online digital marketing course by mastering the necessary and changing resources.

6. Keep updated

As the field of digital marketing becomes highly dynamic, you need to keep up with new developments, strategies and resources. Additionally, the competences may be obsolete. Digital marketing tools will help you continually improve your skills.

7. Building a network

Networking is a key to building company and job partnerships. You will connect with subject matter experts, industry experts, fellow students and similar minded individuals through digital marketing programmes.

Skills to Become a Rockstar in Digital Marketing

The technology is constantly changing and helps advertisers and businessmen to become more knowledgeable of the brand, to meet the target market and eventually to facilitate sales and profit.

Unfortunately, not many business owners or experts have the right skills to succeed in their business. We do not however offer the best e-mail marketing service and produce content targeted to their market. Their multimedia ads tend to their viewers half-baked.

Fret not. Through persistence, hard work and dedication, digital marketing skill can be mastered. You will learn the unique skills to execute powerful digital marketing strategies for your brand.

Here are the perfect skills for becoming a rockstar in digital marketing:

1. Data analytics

Nowadays, applications for data analytics are commonly used, which allow advertisers to identify and deliver the best messaging to reach consumers. Data analytics include the use of new practical and technological technology for collecting and analyzing extensive data collection from your target market's different online experiences.

Such connections take different forms, such as online transactions, accessed information, search queries and other business-related online files. Remember that if you don't know how to analyze the data for your consumers and develop marketing strategies for your company, any form of consumer data will be worthless.

In addition to data analysis, data is filtered to delete inaccurate, duplicated and missing database records. As a digital marketer, you will periodically delete outdated and redundant data from your inventory so that incorrect targeting decisions are not made.

2. Writing and Editing Skills

Content is central to digital marketing, writing and editing skills. The composition and editing of blog posts and landing pages are more than the output of documents. The aim is to communicate with and encourage the target audience to take the correct messaging.

Of course, any digital marketer must have a specific and well-written copy and content. Nevertheless, the innovative use of SEO keywords will help optimize the framework. Optimization by keywords can allow your search engine content to be able to be found by your audience.

Consider it an aim to create products that are always edible. It ensures that the information is still important to their data requirements if someone discovers it the day after or even two years after the publication date.

3. SEO and SEM Skills

If the right people can't find it, a well-written blog post or email will be worthless. Recall the methods responsible to guide the website through Search Engine Optimization (SEO) and Search engine marketing (SEM). A deeper understanding of this ensures that your marketing plans are properly applied.

The Algorithm of Google is constantly upgrading, and it is of current value to use important unique keywords. With every day the world's web is becoming more and more populated, it is important to keep up to date with all recent algorithm changes and search ranking variables. In their content-creation and marketing approaches, advertisers also need to understand these technologies strategically in order to attract and involve people.

4. Hearing skills

One common mistake brand tends to focus too much on content creation and promotion. As such, the consumers, which should be the evangelists or sponsors of their business, do not have an excellent relationship.

The successful development of material is based on data that you collect and analyze to enable the target audience to decide the information that they need and how they want to provide it to them. If you want to be a great digital marketer, you know that your products are critical for their architecture, knowledge and promotion.

So how can you better express your marketing message to consumers? Through vision.

Listen to social media and the way your target audience communicates on your name, products and services. Social listening also gives you an insight into how the target market views your rivals.

5. Email Marketing Skills

Even if email marketing is an old practice, it is still one of the most successful ways of building a good connection with your clients. So consider the best email marketing tool outside the box.

You must know and understand the right tools, metrics and tactics in order for you to build a dynamic email marketing strategy. This will include the study of click speeds, site navigation recognition and e-mail promotions.

6. CRM Skills

Management of customer relationships requires techniques to track and optimize customer experience. You will engage with your clients on a personal and emotional basis and strengthen your company by hearing about their relationships and perceptions.

To improve your customer service training, you will need a set of skills to support you: Empathy. Begin to ask yourself if you were a client, how are you going to be commercialised? How would you like to get to and talk to?

Good skills in conversation–each customer is special. It's also special how they do it. Nonetheless, it is easier to work out a lot with them when you learn how to connect well with different people.

7. Social media

The social media world has become one of the main sites for public talks. You can use that power as a digital marketer to involve people with your business and let people know your product or service.

You may already be familiar with social media ever since it first existed you have regularly used it. But an effective digital marketer recognizes that social media is more than just regular and consistent messaging.

While businesses now use social media to engage their target consumers, the networks have evolved significantly to satisfy their digital marketing needs. Social media ads, tweets, hashtags, corporate accounts, communities, etc. are available. Currently, a lot has to be learned.

Community management also promotes the expertise of social media as it includes taking the opportunity to develop a better relationship with your clients.

8. Skills for social media

Social media isn't as easy as it used to be. This takes more than creating a business profile, using the proper hashtags or sharing fun and relevant content daily to your target market.

For example, Facebook Ads provides marketers and advertisers a robust ad-making tool. But, how do you guarantee that you use it?

You could invest more than you need without a good understanding of how social media advertisements function and not reach the right audience.

Tools like Facebook Insights, learn and develop skills in the fields of OCPM bidding, innovative ad innovation, granular personalized targeting and social media research.

9. Basic design expertise

Text can not be everything in the marketing world. This requires a visual appearance well-designed. This doesn't mean you have to be a rockstar in Photoshop. But if the graphic artist does not alter the visual appearance of your content, it is time-consuming. Hen it's easier to communicate what your content is going to show you have basic knowledge of design principles.

10. Mobile Marketing

Researchers say that nearly half of B2B customers study their mobile devices when operating, while 51 percent of consumers find a new business while they search their smartphones.

Since the rise of mobile ads doesn't seem to stop, many businesses and social media platforms now find new ways to reach users on their mobile phones.

You now need to figure out how to create web advertising and how you can make your company more dependent on customers ' smartphones.

It's not for everybody's digital marketing. Nevertheless, these competencies can be taught. You will take advantage of all the knowledge and resources you need. It's about investing time and energy mastering these 10 key skills and you become a rock star in digital marketing.

The Main Concerns With Digital Marketing to the Mass Market

In the communications field, digital media are becoming influential these days, but the question is how far they reach the general public. The growth of the digital marketing industry has led to a rise in the demand for new-age digital marketers and digital marketing courses. While digital marketing is definitely producing great results in the industry, how successful is it really in the mass market? Let's see: it's an undifferentiated market which includes a huge community of end users with a widely diverse background and population. The consumer market is not split into lifestyles or interests, as opposed to a niche market. If a company produces a commodity that is suitable for a significant number of consumers, a mass market effect is said to exist. Would it not be amazing if businesses could generate this appeal for all their goods on the mass market?

Mass market digital marketing:

As opposed to mass media outlets like TV or newspapers, digital marketing offers affordable access to the mass market. This seeks to categorize a part of the mass market into several categories depending on their backgrounds and desires.

Digital marketing is more a' micro-marketing' than mass marketing which is targeted at the wider range of consumers in its entirety, and divides consumers based on different parameters. The retail industry as a whole can not be reached by digital marketing.

Digital marketing issues for the mass market:

1. **Visibility:** Scholars have demonstrated the very limited approach to digital marketing that relies not on long-term consequences. To order to gain a greater visibility, advertisers can replace the targeting with advanced mass marketing. That's a very interesting point of view.

Nonetheless, segmentation and targeting, primarily used in digital marketing, gives the exposure of your name and the right audience in the right way. Which successful, however, is it on the wider mass market?

Targeted marketing, which leads to higher exposure, engagement and sales levels, is without question being used by brands. Nonetheless, tailored campaigns and mass marketing tactics should be the right mix to stay relevant on the market. To order to provide greater brand pertinence and market exposure, wider marketing and Micromarketing approaches should be used together.

2. **Mass targeting:** No one size fits all the new world strategy. Facebook, Instagram, Snapchat and more digital channels tend to reduce the market to smaller groups. Of examples, the main focus of a new product is to reach mass consciousness. While for proven goods, current knowledge needs to be turned into a kind of practice and the customer is urged to buy. All cases involve unconventional campaign approaches.

3. **Effectiveness:** You need absolute clarity about what you want to do in order to measure the effectiveness of a digital marketing campaign. In terms of scale, dedication and conversion, every digital medium is special. You may be shocked to see that performance on certain digital channels is really difficult to measure. In reality, last year, Facebook admitted how long videos on the website are being viewed by up to 80 people.

Modern metrics of performance are more critical than ever. More CEOs advise the company and Google to boost their market efficiency by identifying and applying a system of accurate metrics.

4. **Careful reach:** It is high time that we stress the focus which takes more than "visibility" into account. Social media and other digital channels would certainly help you find several brand names, but they lead to real time sales rather than just seeing them?

Marketers will examine the number of views, their scope and the total watch period that their campaign produced. However it's important to reach, but it's not really strong enough on its own.

5. **Optimization:** Now that we have the opportunity to tweak marketing campaigns in real time through digital marketing, advertisers need to avoid the tentation of making knee-jerk decisions, which tend to take them away from success. How you measure, and how efficiously you track, is important to know, so that you can change your strategies as necessary.

The amount of data on digital channels is massive and celebrated that companies can carry out effective marketing campaigns. There's no question about its immaculate development with the growing demand on the market for certification programs for online digital marketing and employment.

CHAPTER FIVE

Ways Digital Has Changed Business Forever

We're a new technology-driven society. That's why nations have not running water but smartphones themselves. They're there. Digital marketing has an incredible impact on the relationships, jobs, recruitment and lifestyle of people.

As such, today businesses need to be focused on how they can optimize brand awareness and impact by using the digital universe. In this blog, I discuss the main ways digital marketing has evolved and the way businesses and brands work continues to change.

- ✓ **Quick communication**

Nowadays it could be like roulette roulette wheel communicating with potential customers.

The Roulette Ball reflects the marketing message of the organization, which rotates and bounces as the wheel turns before it finally reaches a location (i.e., a client). Social media serves as the axis, allowing businesses to communicate and to promote products, services and clear communications in a public space.

But a new player is in the pool, and before leaving the port companies need to figure out how to sail on the proverbial boats. A fifth of all apps downloaded are discarded, according to the Economist, after one use and instant messaging buckles the trend.

One-on - one conversations are now on blast, as is private chat communities. Facebook messenger has over 900 million users worldwide and surveys have shown that young people already spend more time on chat apps than on actual social networks. Smart companies develop methods of communication with potential customers and communicate with them by these types of applications to tap into this vast market.

✓ **Overload content**

How much content is transmitted through social media and messaging applications? The response is immense, so enormous that the word material shock was given. 3.3 million users post on Facebook every 60 seconds and 29 million messages are sent on Whatsapp. It means advertisers have their work cut off if the people who use these apps are to consider their message and name.

Rolex is an excellent example of a traditional company that uses imagination to convey its marketing message to consumers and prospects. This could pose problems with keeping the brand new as a brand with 112 years of history. Nevertheless, this is solved by producing high quality and glamorous product images that show their classic feel and durability. Using trendy and sleek pictures, he yells class and consumers by highlighting his goods and time-free message through his photos, videos and editorial work.

✓ **Information drives**

Modern technology allows advertisers to acquire tremendous visibility into their customers. Organizations should however know how, where and when such details can be used.

Understanding the metrics which are the most important for the success of the company–understanding what your corporation wants to accomplish is the secret to the effect of results. The important thing is to be very particular about the market outcomes and to understand how the statistics are calculated and how it impacts the larger organization.

The variety of technology and platforms ensures that a company must concentrate on the ones with which the client is engaged in a meaningful fashion and realize which consumer channels are to pay for. Looks and feedback that seem relevant but what matters is the dedication that creates a customer-brand partnership.

Using computational data processing workers–without the ability of learning what to do with the data at home, all the data in the world is worthless.

Data analysis is what can guide an organization and help them understand a consumer's actions and discomfort.

The vast amount of data in cyberspace makes it difficult for any company to make real change–the production of personalized advertising and the consumer focus. The key is to know who the target audience is and to produce offerings that catch their interest and inspire them to participate.

✓ Transparency demands

Consumers want to learn the businesses with which they communicate and shop from in the digital world today. Brands must be straightforward to build trust and show their identity online and the values of the brand. This is especially relevant because customers want to know exactly what they eat in food products.

A recent study Insight offers just 12% of customers trust companies in advertising and looking for information on the company elsewhere, while 67% agree that it is up to the manufacturer.

Of honest and freely speaking firms, 94 percent of customers continue to be faithful to a trustworthy brand, while 73 per cent would be willing to pay more for a product that provides them.

The demand for consistency in the labeling of foodstuffs applies to many aspects of business from how its workers manage their contributions to society and societies. This will be understood and aware of information, whether good, bad or nasty, by digital management.

✓ Fostering intimacy

Businesses can gain a huge amount of the data they can gather from potential customers. The clever businesses use this data to produce extremely personal marketing messages and it is consumed by the younger generation.

Cultural changes and the understanding of others continue to inspire thousands of years. It makes personalization a powerful tool, because 85% of consumers are likely to purchase a product when the message is optimized and publicly accepted.

For mark its 20th birthday, the organization has analyzed the data it gathers and discovered fascinating insights on the voyages of its clients. The outcome was an e-mail camp using interactive photos and connections to tell the story of each passenger from their first flight to those in future flights and to incorporate some interesting details about their travel conduct.

The result was open rates of more than 100% over normal easyJet newsletter with 25% higher rates. Across social media the response was overwhelmingly positive, with 685,000 people reaching more than 1,1 million views and a total of over minutes. 7.5% of the consumers who received the email made a reservation in the next 30 days in all regions.

✓ A new generation of influencers

Social media and video platforms such as YouTube have empowered "ordinary" people to gain incredible influence. Companies no longer have to employ celebrities to endorse their brands and draw millions of people to their items.

Normal people without any other qualifications than many social media followers now have the ability to influence them by merely promoting a particular product. Although micro-influencers –those below 100,000 have more power and higher levels of dedication than well-known individuals.

Brands, mindful of these emerging influencers, engaged influencers in educating and involving customers. Take for example Coca-Cola, which switched to house influencers in their own YouTube channel, Coke TV, through dependency on the use of influencers.

✓ Catch-up play

Digital technology is evolving at an extremely fast rate, sometimes overnight. Without ceasing to step forward, these changes require department-wide staff to be flexible, to coordinate and to keep progress most critically up-to-date, to evolve and to leverage these changes for the good of the company.

It is a smart way to achieve this by keeping schooling, as and when workers need it. Employees can be vigilant in their understanding of what's happening to consider how their companies can use these transition to their advantage through training in the new and most applicable technology, tactics and techniques.

Take an example of IBM. We also launched a digital sales pilot program that turned their traditional sales team into digital sellespersons in full knowledge of the changing landscape. The pilot has proven to be so effective that its distribution capability, growth boost and changed thought and the role of the project across internet networks are evolving internationally. It has now been adopted

In turn, organizations across sectors need to be mindful of the pace of change and engage in training and growth programs to ensure that their workers are at the forefront of digital marketing and sales.

✓ Encourage innovation

The new landscape has pushed companies to experiment with innovative ways of reaching out to their clients and communicating with them. Most businesses have had to be innovative in the face of disrupters to pursue steps in which they can perform. For example, financial institutions needed new ways to engage and impact clients, in the face of stiff competition from PayPal and Google Wallet.

The best way to achieve this has been for many to work with potential disruptors with fresh and new ideas. Innovative centers are able to embrace the new digital world and help serve their customers. Key players in the industry include Barclays and JP Morgan.

Initiating an engineering center in Asia Pacific demonstrated HSBC's creativity in designing digital and mobile banking systems of the next decade. The goal is to strengthen the bank's strategic innovation program in order to maximize international reach and connectivity.

✓ Make Brands More Human

Because of its success and impact, social media marketing should be a focus for every brand, because consumers must believe and appreciate the business of which they shop.

Apple is one of the best examples of an organisation going reduces to nature. Strategic messaging means that Apple has millions of people to buy their goods before they are launched! brand conscience is the ultimate of their consumers.

We achieve this using live streaming events which result in hundreds of loyal customers thinking that we contribute to the brand's journey and, as such, Apple needs to invest in a kind of« cultural radar» by keeping abreast of evolving technology and platforms, together with investments in digital talent, which are capable of understanding them. Brands capable of embracing and adapting can fly in front of competition.

The Scope of Digital Marketing in 2020

The way consumers consume information has developed over the years. Radio advertisement led to TV advertising which became obviously everywhere the digital marketing techniques that we see today.

Although TV remains an area of prime exposure for many businesses, the move into digital marketing has made it possible for marketers to enter a global market through online advertising. With this sector rising at a quick global rate, it is no surprise that there have also been more digital marketing employment. Here you can look at the reasons for digital marketing and the career paths in the industry.

1. Why is digital marketing Lean Toward?

Industries are attempting to maintain sales flow with new marketing techniques, either by adding internet elements to brick-and-mortar stores or by integrating various digital marketing strategies to enter the lucrative online market.

Since most consumers now use smartphones and online research tools when making purchases, digital marketing strategies for these companies have become necessary if their respective target audience is to be drawn. Nonetheless, smartphones and online research are not the only reasons businesses have turned to digital marketing worldwide. We use these techniques to better target the online and mobile parts of the market— and many have huge ROIs.

✓ *Ease of Consumer Targeting*

Digital marketing makes it easier for marketers to use data for their target audiences based on factors such as gender, age, place, preferences and employment, and to re-engage potential customers with different methods and messaging in the consumer group already familiar with their brand. Online marketing certifications are even developed to allow digital marketers to master this technology.

- ✓ *Low investment; a high return*

Marketing costs are 61% smaller per user for digital or inbound technologies than traditional marketing. Companies who promote social media, check paid for, and use other marketing tactics have considerably reduced their spending on their promotions, largely due to the fact that many employ pay-per-click (PPC) techniques to minimize and increase their own costs. In fact, their ROI is not only higher, but also higher.

- ✓ *Mobile Users Reach*

Today there are 8.6 billion wireless networks, which are more than the population of the world. Since most smartphones today have internet access, businesses can meet potential customers anywhere, anywhere and even more quickly than ever.

2. The Digital Marketing Scope

In recent years digital marketing has grown with 88 percent of companies that use social media as a main advertisement target.

- ✓ ***B2B:*** To generate leads, B2B marketers rely on web traffic but also are active on social media platforms like LinkedIn and Twitter. They also often rely on PPC campaigns to reach target audiences inexpensively.

- ✓ ***B2C***: B2C marketers focus on improving brand awareness and attracting customers to their websites and products using social platforms like Facebook, Twitter, Instagram, and Pinterest.

In addition to social media, businesses are using paid search, email marketing, and other methods to reach new audiences.

3. Digital Marketing 2020 and beyond

Each year more and more businesses enter the world and new technologies are being created and digital marketing trends continue. Here are some developments into 2020 that will help to shape this region.

✓ *Influencers of social media*

Inserts in all industries communicate with influencers of social media to boost their brands. It proved to be a successful digital marketing tactic, primarily because customers tend to believe that other buyers do not really want their goods to be marketed in actual companies. Expect more companies to use these influencers to boost sales in 2020 and beyond.

✓ *Video Remains King*

in 2020, video continues to be a dominant tactic, as digital advertisers take advantage of the short attention span and ability to watch videos instead of reading. Despite 74% of consumers in the world watching such videos every week online, live video still has an important role to play in linking customers and companies to boost their engagement. The video as well as video sharing services are provided by most social media channels in the present day to satisfy advertiser and customer demand.

✓ *Artificial Intelligence*

Online marketers have gathered more efficient data analyzes to allow them to change their consumer journeys further. For AI, projects, all about an individual, and outcomes that will most certainly cater to particular segments of the population, are programmed to understand. AI gives consumers also a more individual experience, giving them tailored assistance at every point of the purchasing process. Part of this can be done by automating advertisements with programmatic advertisement for different viewers.

✓ *Improved and augmented reality*

Through their marketing strategies advertisers will begin to use Augmented Reality (AR) and Virtual Reality (VR) through order to increase brand awareness and customer demand. Brands such as Starbucks, Nivea and Volkswagen have carried out successful campaigns to provide consumers with a visceral experience that ties them closer with their marks and items.

4. Digital marketing careers

Digital marketers will observe and integrate these patterns into their strategies. As a credible, powerful, tangible, and user-friendly medium, they focus on digital marketing–and while businesses continue to explore the online market for greater access, more jobs are available than ever to satisfy these needs.

A digital marketing manager's average salary tops $74,000 annually. Many high paying positions include social media marketing managers, PPC practitioners, digital marketing advisors, and SEO specialists. In the digital marketing room, bloggers and YouTubers will effectively compose and vlog.

Research in the digital marketing industry is widely available, but to excel in the field a strong knowledge of these approaches and strategies is necessary. Thankfully, vendors such as Simplilearn provide a DMS system to support digital marketers in accordance with one of the fastest growing disciplines in the nation. With dedicated online learning, marketers and learners can initiate and sustain successful campaigns through social media, PPC, SEO, web analytics, emails, content and mobile marketing tactics.

Tips on How Digital Marketing Can Increase Your Revenue

The Internet has become a popular space for people to interact, communicate and work. The majority of companies have moved online for most of their activities. They use all sorts of tricks to boost digital marketing traffic on their pages.

To follow a plan for digital marketing? Secondly, it's very cost-effective web marketing. This makes it popular with entrepreneurs of various scales. Even though you are a beginner, you still have the strong chance to run a successful marketing strategy without wasting fortune. When you start growing the business. Looks like a businessman's fantasy, isn't it?

The next issue is how to use social media to generate more income for a client.

There are several ways to increase the money you can use but the following are the top five:

1. Optimisation of websites

Do you have an official site for your company? If you do, you know how much it will cost to build. A good website is easy to navigate and user-friendly. It is also well-formatted –designed by SEO. Engines for quest. It should également be regularly checked and revised, otherwise competitive web sites which are optimized will dim the company in search lists.

You must use trendy keywords and phrases and place them dynamically in your page material to outspread the majority of your website. Specific methods such as ad-words are used for analyzing and assessment of prominence and potential search queries high on the web pages of these keywords. If your link is in the front pages, there are more chances for consumers to see your products resulting in more purchases.

2. Using Google My Business tool

Google Business App is one of the methods used to increase business awareness for professional Digital Marketers. It is offered for free, which ensures that anyone can use it in browsing Google sites or maps to improve their visibility.

The tool works well when you have a physical store with physical connections and you have a heavy traffic in your company. The approach is highly effective for Google My Business as the chances for nearby customers to come to see the store improve into more profits.

3. Email nurturing

You must have sent unsolicited e-mails from your mailbox to invite you to buy items when you have an email address. If you have no experience in the promotional content, these e-mails can be irritating. Nonetheless, you can position yourself as a trusted partner by supporting product and unique beneficiaries in a timely manner if you excel in developing your brand and use email services as a digital marketing tool.

Since these e-mails are not to be sent to everyone, only the clients and prospective purchasers found by lead generation tests or by subscribers to your newsletters should be e-mailed. The better the conversion rate you advertise for this party.

4. Company profiles in social media

This is one of the best digital advertising tactics in today's world, because many people spend most of their time surfing and keeping up with their friends on social media. Some of them just sign in and see what's going on in the world.

How about placing the ads strategically on its walls? You might wonder how you can make your goods freely available to customers based on their interests and browsing history, but if you are in touch with social media companies like Facebook.

Instead, you can put your goods on your website if you are interested in several media backers and consumers can purchase them if they are interested.

5. Using marketing tracking tools

Traders using various sales-enhancing policies; others pay for search engines such as Google to post their products on their websites while others use their large online community to market their products.

Regardless of your plan, you should avoid throwing more money at it if you know it's not working, because you may lose a lot but won't. Only with a tracking tool is this feasible. It can cost extra money, but it's important.

Not only are these digital marketing tactics used to raise business revenue, they are also some of the strongest.

Smart Ways for Bringing New Life To Your Business

Would you think your business doesn't expand enough? Want to get your business a new life? Would you like your business to add value without burning a hole in your pocket?

A new life for an existing company can seem like a daunting and costly mission. Nevertheless, note that tiny is great when it comes to giving the business a new taste.

Here are the recommendations to bring your company to new life:

1. Build upon a brand identity

A brand logo is one of the best marketing tools available for both small and large businesses. Based upon a brand identity A logo creates an interesting re-call appeal for the company and is the best way to improve sales. It is one of the best ways to rejuvenate your business, goods, and services. By using a catchy tag-line to accompany the slogan, the identity will be boosted in new energy.

Sometimes it also helps create a new identity for the company by modifying the original logo.

Several firms are now using tailor-made brands to generate new value in their products. Companies such as iCustomlabel will help you create a wide range of products such as wine labels, personalized placemats, beer labels, water bottle labels and even cigar label. Personalized eye-catching stickers can be used to attract potential customers.

Decorating the business with the logo is also a simple way to give the office a new look. During the holiday season, a number of companies also offer personalized items to new and loyal customers.

2. Social Media

Social media marketing among businesses, especially small and medium-sized companies, is quickly gaining prominence. Social media presence is huge such as Facebook, Snapchat, Twitter and What's App.

Organizations will harness the interests of customers around the world through social media platforms. Social media marketing isn't at all expensive. There's not much experience available, too. Repeating potential customers in different parts of the world helps with daily updates, forums and posts.

Most organizations remain opposed to social media marketing because of lack of knowledge or lack of time. You may consider working with social media administrators in such situations. These specialists are trained in digital marketing. You will owe the social networking a professional lift. The complexities and techniques of social media marketing are well versed. You can produce more supporters at very nominal cost and like it for your company.

3. Collaborations

it's worth working with other firms several times. You will partner with book clubs, students and animals clubs, for example, if you are a coffee shop owner and provide their café with space for activities.

You should try to build your connections with schools, universities, animal clubs, book clubs, art clubs, literary societies, poetry clublings and golf clubs, to name a few, depending on your products and services. This may not lead to immediate revenue growth, but a daily and loyal clientele would certainly be created.

For turn, you can try to offer local charities products and services. Some businesses now sell personalized stickers for free products at local fairs and festivals. It helps attract customers who haven't used the goods but now are ready to try them just because they don't have to pay for them.

4. Map yourself

You know it will show you the best pizza sites around you, if you type pizza on Google Maps? More and more users are now seeking products and services through apps such as Google Maps.

It is important that online platforms such as Google Maps, Foursquare, Facebook Business, TripAdvisor and Yelp your business, product, or service is readily available. Because you offer the best goods at the most competitive prices, you can lose sales simply because your online presence is not strong.

Clear reviews are extremely important for your company to be accepted in the world today. You should persuade loyal customers, friends and family to post on various online mediums good reviews or recommendations about your business.

It is critical that customer reviews are honest and realistic. Always post manufactured products and be too perfect for real feedback as the majority of readers can read bogus and misleading recommendations. Flawed comparisons will in the long run harm the company's reputation.

5. A great website

Every company in the world today is incomplete without a good website to support it. Three I's a good website, mind. Mind. An engaging, informative and interesting website is always superior.

The application is continuously incorporated by an interactive website. It offers a good mix of graphics, videos and photos for a great online experience. It must have comprehensive and informative detail on the goods, programs, promotions and special packages of your company.

It should also address persons with particular needs and be mobile-friendly. The F5 key on a computer and laptop keyboards is required by companies today. Just one click to refresh it easily! It is important to remember the max with all businesses: "There is no distinction between winning things. They do different things. "We do various things.

Marketing Lessons to Succeed in 2020

For the last 10 years branding and promotion have been going, but every year people learn new things. This is because messaging is always evolving and different from each company is important and efficient.

1. Use your own social media

Too many social media managers are so committed to the use of social media by businesses but not people. They forget what people really like and refer to ordinary people. Individual users are the audience you meet on social media. Use and enjoy social media. Post personal stuff and see what connections are having. Remember the material with which you are associated. You will hear about what is really interesting about ordinary people.

2. Know your priorities and your reasons

I worked with many clients who just want to change things to change them. You want to make a difference in the nature or quality of something, and the logic is, they just want to "change something," or "say it would be more effective." You have a purpose and a tangible goal to obtain from this transition before you change it. Make the change, check it, and retain or remove it depending on the results.

3. Intended post

There may be a considerable pressure to hold up in the space of digital content. Whether it is blog posts, videos, social media or emails, everybody's pouring out so much material that you feel the pressure to keep delivering. Quality is important, while accuracy is important. Don't make shit. Don't make shit. You're more upset than you have done something. Scale back onto your material schedule if it's too much, so that you can do less and more purposefully.

4. Makes things Simplier

There's a temptation to add more flashy stuff because we think it's more effective. So we add more words, more graphics, and more features. But that only creates more options and confusion for your audience. Whether it's on your website, emails, or print marketing, keep it clear and concise. Ask if an element needs to be there, and how it helps the customer make a decision.

5. Repurpose and recycle

Development of fresh content for several channels is exhausting. Blogs, videos, podcasts and all social media platforms are available. I'd dial myself down on a specific platform if I didn't have time. An simple way to generate less materials and still satisfy the distribution criteria of each site is to repurpose and recycle a single piece of content in several formats over the year.

6. Speak to your target market, not to your current audience

They always follow a different or modern multicultural group. For order to succeed in the future, you need to make this change. But when we create different messages to approach their desired demographic, they are concerned that their existing audience is alienated. But they try to find a balanced backdrop to cater to both hands, but don't repeat one. Speak to whom you want to meet preferably. It could damage you by losing your current market now, but it will benefit you if you link to the clients you wish for.

7. People buy products and not features

Companies that claim that they have a great product and that many times they do, but that with all their ads, they don't see any revenue. Also because they don't respond to the concerns of their clients. We still try to solve a dilemma when somebody buys it. Brands talk about how great their product is but don't translate to sales because they don't think about how it addresses challenges for their clients. Don't launch a product; offer a solution.

8. People buy emotions, not stuff

Brands that consider sales difficult fight with a similar error. While consumers have a great product and a fantastic approach, they have many options. You're not going to choose a brand that is what you get, but how you look. People decide how their feelings are influenced and how their personality is shaped. Let the company feel good and confident.

9. Address it with the company and not yourself

I notice a lot of consumers talk about themselves when I check email or website content. They're going to say' We do this,' or' This is our offering.' You won't interest you if you're not involved in you. Switch the marketing language to talk to your customers directly.

10. Messaging is more important than fonts and colors:

How much I go with clients over minor details is shocking. I recognize why their branding identity is often covered by marketers. Yet small design changes do not alter when they reach a plateau and battle production. The message that is conveyed to your consumers is more relevant.

11. Many sessions are meaningless

Most of them are time wasted. This normally takes an average of one hour and a half to two hours for weekly meetings. They continue with a non-work talk for about 15 minutes. The meeting leader will usually make an announcement around 10-15 minutes by the manager or supervisor. During this conference, they will go through all of them and refresh their job. Occasionally, 2-3 people talk about a particular topic and everyone else without any participation is watching and listening. It's a matter of time. The workshop would typically be extended, the next week or in smaller groups for unresolved talks. Nearly all data can be spread via e-mail. Don't get together to share information. Provide fewer gatherings to solve the problems, include only those who need to be there and tell them what they will do in advance.

12. Your time is a bento box and not the buffet platform

We sometimes add tasks to our work lists without allocating the right time. It delays existing projects and places them on the back burner. Tasks take time. Tasks take time. You don't have a table wall to stack up on jobs. Your time is a bento box with only limited space to fill. When you add additional tasks, you need to know which other tasks will be delayed or eliminated.

13. Automation and delegation

Individuals tend to wear multiple hats and do anything for small organizations or individual business owners. But as they grow they adhere to that patterns and do little repetitive tasks that shouldn't take their time. Technology and programs that can simplify a lot of your duties and transfer your job to other people will be discovered as soon as possible.

14. Go forward:

The urgent trend prevents future growth. Yet many companies are doing that. They do stuff every day, every week, and get them done just in time. Nevertheless, it does not give time to assess performance or to create better strategies. Even if it appears that you have to postpone those marketing plans, plan ahead and do things in advance. You're going to have much more space.

15. Employing someone is the best investment in growth

The most costly of all companies is usually labour, and bosses and self-employed people try to keep things thin by doing all their jobs themselves. Nonetheless, the time they spend to do that work prevents them from doing more important work which could help the company to expand. When you have the ability to hire workers or consultants to offload jobs that you actually do not need to do, so that you can work on things at the highest level that affect your business's future.

16. Consider always about scaling

Small businesses and self-employed people are used to doing things in a certain way and can be extremely inefficient. But because they're so small, they don't know it. The low volume then makes them go that way. It can be the production and distribution process, client relations or even office activities. And, if they were to weigh, they could never keep up and often that is what keeps them from scaling. Take a look at some of the longest-ranging activities and think how 10 times the number of customers would be possible. Seek ways to improve productivity so that you can expand your market more quickly.

17. Cash to lose on risk

Nobody likes to waste money. Successful companies must guarantee they get some kind of return whatever they invest. Even items that seem to be more superficial like workplace bonuses, with the goal of increasing productivity, are done for employee morality.

Risk is part of any venture, but some companies are so risk-averse that it does not allow them to take the necessary measures to expand. What benefits often are businesses budgeting and investing a certain amount just for costs and anticipating no return. It frees them from becoming bolder. You might buy new appliances, invest on advertising, or try a new program. However you believe your company might probably expand, but you are not totally confident. A budget for "risks" gives you confidence in making progress.

18. Be vigilant about patterns rather than fads

They will look at fads that are sometimes long ago and insist that these things are done because the other brands have looked popular. We don't know it is often a one-off or a lot of money has been spent on little ROI, or it's a short time hyped-up case. Nonetheless, patterns are consumer phenomena that last for many years or longer. We are worth following and checking, and if you get on at the right time, it could be very useful. See what is a long-term phenomenon and what is only a short-term fad and be prepared to easily adapt and change.

CONCLUSION

Digital marketing is a broad term which involves advertisement, support and reinforcement of companies ' online presence through digital platforms. Digital advertising, e-mail marketing, content marketing, pay-per-click brochures and much more are some of the digital strategies under the umbrella of Digital Marketing. Digital marketing helps exact results to be collected in real time, as does other off-line marketing efforts. Of example, it is almost impossible to estimate the number of people who turned to this page and paid attention to this ad if you put ads into the newspaper. Through digital marketing, you can calculate every part of your marketing efforts with ease.

Users spend a lot of time on the internet today. Over recent years, the rise over social networking sites has brought more users to their desktops, computers and mobile devices. In recent surveys, an engaged Facebook user is estimated to spend an hour on Facebook on an average each day. People spend more time now than in the last decade on the internet. The Internet has become an integral part of many people's lives. This condition is also being used to the fullest for digital marketing.

Digital media is ubiquitous to the extent wherever and whenever consumers encounter results. The days have gone where you sent the messages to people about your things or governments and what you needed to know.

Digital media is a constantly growing medium of entertainment, advertising, shopping and social communication. Today, consumers are not just focused with what the company does in regards to their profile. In fact, they are likely to trust you as well. Customers need products they can trust, organisations that represent them, personalized and meaningful communications to deliver custom-built approaches to their needs and inclinations.

To order to make it clear, digital marketing is literally the selling of any internet products or services. It's a kind of marketing' new-age' infrastructure that is different from traditional or modern marketing programs. The idea that digital marketing has the luxury of controlling all facets of your marketing strategy makes it different from traditional marketing. And this tracking will, of course, be carried out in real time.

www.ingramcontent.com/pod-product-compliance
Lightning Source LLC
Chambersburg PA
CBHW070423220526
45466CB00004B/1524